An American Initiative

An American Initiative

Toward a Sino-American Entente

John Clayborne Epps

John Clayborne Epps
15 March 2009

San Salvador
El Salvador

VANTAGE PRESS
New York

FIRST EDITION

Published by Vantage Press, Inc.
516 West 34th Street, New York, New York 10001

Manufactured in the United States of America
ISBN: 0-533-11925-1

Library of Congress Catalog Card No.: 96-90191

0 9 8 7 6 5 4 3 2 1

For my parents, the President, and peace on Earth

Contents

Contents

An American Initiative

I / Executive Summary: Toward a Sino-American Entente

A cooperative China could help ease international tensions, contribute to the resolution of regional conflicts, support American military deployments and diplomatic initiatives intended to ensure stability in troubled regions, and join constructively in the new international regimes being formed to bolster cooperative security.[1]
—Dr. Harry Harding, The George Washington University

Of the five permanent members of the United Nations Security Council, the People's Republic of China is the only one not to have actively participated as a principal negotiator in a Middle East peace conference. This truth is thrust into sharp relief when considered within the context of another reality: that the longevity and scope of China's formal diplomacy in the region equals or surpasses that of the other four permanent Security Council members. As Lillian Craig Harris explained in her authoritative book, *China Considers the Middle East:*

In 651, diplomatic relations were formally established between China and Arabia, and over the next 100 years various other Arab Muslim rulers delegated more than a dozen embassies to China.[2]

This analysis advocates the convening of an international conference—to be co-chaired by the United States

1

and the People's Republic of China—toward the resolution of regional conflicts. As U.S. Senator Bill Bradley, a New Jersey Democrat, explained during a Senate speech on 18 May 1994:

> Because China is a veto-wielding permanent member of the United Nations Security Council, Chinese cooperation is vital for the American global agenda from Bosnia to Iraq.[3]

The regional conflicts to be resolved, however, can be determined in deliberations prior to the adoption of this initiative. The ongoing conflict in Bosnia is the preeminent candidate.

> Another civil war—the continuing conflict in the Sudan—has most recently been waged for 14 years between: 1) the Arabic-speaking Muslims whose northern regime attempts to rule the nation; and 2) the black-African Christian rebels in the south.[4]

The motivation driving this initiative is one that differs from that of resolving regional conflicts: the inducement of greater flexibility by the Chinese leadership regarding the PRC's policy on human rights. That an international conference might induce Chinese cooperation on human-rights questions was inferred by John Shattuck, the U.S. Assistant Secretary of Sstate for Democracy, Human Rights and Labor. Mr. Shattuck's remarks were made in Alexandria, Virginia, on 18 July 1994, in an address to the Asia Foundation's Center for Asian Pacific Affairs:

> The U.S. government will maintain human rights as an essential part of our engagement with China. Among the elements of our forward-looking human rights approach there are facilitating access by the Chinese people to the

world's commerce in information and ideas, **working on a multilateral basis to promote human rights,** engaging with the business community, and helping foster civil society in China.[5] (Emphasis added)

The proposed conference mechanism and seating arrangement—which were conceived in 1981 and formally copywritten in 1991—are presented in this section. The conference is presented herewith, so that policymakers in Congress, the Commerce Department, the State Department, and the White House can consider it as an option. The relevance of such an initiative to current policy was clarified by Secretary of State Warren Christopher on 28, July 1995, during an address to the National Press Club in Washington.

. . . despite the advantages of bilateral contacts, we need to build mechanisms of cooperation on a multilateral basis to assure that the current favorable environment will endure. Thus, the third element our strategy is to build a sound architecture for regional cooperation.[6]

When such an initiative is considered, questions emerge as to China's attitude toward the concept of an international conference dealing directly or indirectly with the Middle Eastern matters. The Chinese—and Asian—attitudes toward the Palestinian and Persian Gulf questions will be the focus of the following sections.

China and the Concept of an International Peace Conference

China's first approval of the concept of a peace conference is said to have emerged in 1977, as the United States and the Soviet Union planned to cochair a proposed Geneva Conference. The Chinese shift in attitude from disapproval to moderation, however, was qualified by the condition that the Palestinian people be afforded "full representation."[7]

The evolution of Chinese attitudes continued in the 1980s, as Lillian Craig Harris explained:

> As the decade opened, China was still convinced that an international peace conference would be manipulated by outsiders to Middle Eastern disadvantage and that the UN was a vehicle for superpower assertiveness. Before the end of the decade China was expressing willingness to participate as a full member of an international peace conference and had praised the UN as "the most important global organization of our time."[8]

On 10 December 1981, the PRC's position on Palestine was further defined by its supportive vote for UNGA Resolution 36/120C. Operative Paragraph One of this resolution decided "to convene, under the auspices of the United Nations, an International Conference on the Question of Palestine."[9] This policy was reinforced in mid-June 1984, when Beijing backed UN Secretary-General Jàvier Pèrez de Cuellar in his campaign to promote an international peace conference. From early 1987 onward, the PRC has promoted the idea of full and active participation in an international conference for the five permanent members of the UN Security Council.[10]

The *sine qua non* of such participation, however, was the normalization of Sino-Israeli diplomatic ties. In July 1987, West German chancellor Helmut Kohl was reported to have acted as a liaison to China so as to convey Israel's desire for diplomatic relations. Then in September 1987—during an unprecedented meeting of Chinese and Israeli foreign ministers at the United Nations—the Israelis are reported to have emphasized the ineluctability of full Sino-Israeli diplomatic relations before Israel could accede to PRC participation in an international peace conference. As Lillian Craig Harris explained:

> Israel had by this time made clear that it would not agree to Chinese participation in a Middle East peace conference before establishment of Sino-Israeli diplomatic ties. When the *Beijing Review* complained in 1988 that Shamir rejected both the proposal for an international peace conference attended by the five permanent members of the United Nations Security Council and the "land for peace" formula, the order of the Chinese sentence indicated which rejection hurt more.[11]

The most comprehensive PRC policy statement on the Middle Eastern question came in October 1989, during PLO Chairman Yasir Arafat's seventh visit to China. At this time, the PRC posited its own proposal for Middle East peace. Through its "Five Step Peace Proposal," China advocated: (1) a political settlement without use of military force; (2) an international Middle East peace conference under UN auspices, attended by the five permanent members of the UNSC and other concerned parties; (3) a direct dialogue between the PLO and Israel; (4) an Israeli withdrawal from occupied territories and guarantees for Israel's security; and (5) an establishment of a state of Palestine that would coexist peacefully with Israel.[12] Chairman Arafat concurred with the PRC plan on 4 October 1989, during a dinner banquet hosted by then-President Yang Shangkun in Beijing:

... an international conference, which must be held under UN auspices and with the participation of all parties to the conflict, including the State of Palestine and Israel and the other Arab states concerned with the conflict, as well as the five permanent members of the UN Security Council, to secure the national and political rights of the Palestinian people, including their rights to self-determination and to establish their independent state.[13]

After explaining that "China's desire to participate in a Middle East peace conference had been evident since the late 1980s," Lillian Craig Harris continued that "China's frequent calls for convening of the international conference stressed participation of the five permanent members of the Security Council." This trend was substantiated on 25 September 1991, during Foreign Minister Qian Qichen's address to the forty-sixth session of the United Nations General Assembly:

China believes that convocation of an international peace conference at an appropriated time under the auspices of the United Nations and with the participation of the five permanent members of the Security Council and all the parties concerned, including the Palestine Liberation Organization (PLO), is the best way leading to a final settlement of the Middle East question.[14]

The absence of formal diplomatic ties with Israel, however, disallowed direct participation by the PRC. On 26 September 1991—during a Beijing news conference—Foreign Ministry spokesman Wu Jianmin stated explicitly that China did "not have plans to establish diplomatic relations with South Africa or Israel."[15] The importance of this factor became evident from 31 October to 4 November 1991, during the Madrid Conference on Middle East Peace:

> The opening of the Middle East peace conference in Madrid in October 1991 let the Chinese know that the time had come. Israel's price for attendance was diplomatic recognition by the Soviet Union and China. Moscow paid this price and the Arabs, seeing peace as the objective, did not complain. **China was the only permanent member of the UN Security Council not included in some form at the opening session of the peace conference.** (Emphasis added)[16]

The elevation of Sino-Israeli relations to the ambassadorial level—on 24 January 1992, during a four-day visit to Beijing by Israeli Foreign Minister David Levy—had set the stage for a conference proposal that features, *inter alios,* all five permanent members of the United Nations Security Council.[17] The conference configuration and mechanism are outlined in the following section.

The Conference Mechanism

This mechanism is designed for the resolution of regional conflicts. It consists of thirteen nations. These thirteen nations subdivide into two panels. The First Panel—totalling eight delegates—might include: (1) Argentina; (2) Venezuela; (3) South Africa; (4) the Palestine Liberation Organization; (5) Israel; (6) Egypt; (7) Cuba; and (8) Brazil. The Final Panel comprises the five permanent members of the UN Security Council: (1) China; (2) France; (3) the United Kingdom; (4) Russia; and (5) the United States. The following page provides a configuration of the seating arrangement.

7

A FULLY-DESIGNATED CONFERENCE CONFIGURATION

THE CHINESE AMBASSADOR

The First Panel
Argentina Venzuela South Africa P.L.O. Israel Egypt Cuba Brazil

THE AMERICAN AMBASSADOR

The Final Panel
China France Russia United Kingdom United States

The mechanism features two peace processes, each with an eight-step, two-month procedure. The process for Conflict B will begin four weeks after the process for Conflict A, to allow a continuous and systematic resolution of the problems by both the First and Final panels. For the sake of clarity, the procedure will be described for four months of the conference mechanism. In this manner, an outline will be given for (1) the first two rounds of the new peace process for Conflict A; and (2) the first one-and-one-half rounds of the new peace process for Conflict B.

Week One

Conflict A: Step One

The Chinese Ambassador inaugurates the conference by opening the peace process for Conflict A. Firstly, the Ambassador presides over reports to the conference regarding: (1) the status of the peacekeeping force; and (2) the current status of Conflict A.

Secondly, the Chinese Ambassador—through a general vote of all thirteen delegates—establishes an itinerary for the resolution of Conflict A. Proposals are accepted from the delegations on the first specified aspect leading to the resolution of Conflict A.

Week Two

Conflict A: Step Two

The Chinese Ambassador leads a general discussion of the proposal for the first specified aspect on the itinerary of Conflict A.

Week Three

Conflict A: Step Three

The Chinese Ambassador conducts a simple majority vote within the First Panel to endorse one of the proposals on the first specified aspect of Conflict A's itinerary.

Week Four

Conflict A: Step Four

The Final Panel will respond in one of two manners. It can accept the decision promulgated by the First Panel. Or, it can request that the American Ambassador conduct a simple majority vote within the Final Panel, in the event of: (1) a 4–4 deadlock within the First Panel; or (2) any dissatisfaction within the Final Panel.

Week Five

Conflict A: Step Five

Should the Final Panel challenge the First Panel's decision, the American Ambassador appeals to the American Ambassador to the United Nations, who will take the issue to the UN Security Council.

Conflict B: Step One

The Chinese Ambassador opens the peace process for the resolution of Conflict B. Firstly, the Ambassador receives reports on the current situation in Conflict B. The Chinese Ambassador then establishes an itinerary—through a general vote of all thirteen delegates—for the resolution of the Conflict B.

Week Six

Conflict A: Step Six

The American Ambassador to the United Nations conducts a vote within the fifteen-member UN Security Council. It will uphold the decision of the First Panel, or, it will enable the Final Panel to resolve—through a simple majority vote of three—the first specific aspect on the itinerary for Conflict A.

Conflict B: Step Two

The Chinese Ambassador conducts a general discussion of

the proposals for the first specified aspect on Conflict B's itinerary.

Week Seven

Conflict A: Step Seven

The Final Panel will respond in one of two manners. It can accept the decision by the UN Security Council, or, it can request that the Chinese Ambassador lead a vote within the Final Panel to overrule the UN Security Council, should the latter uphold the First Panel's decision. A four-to-one decision by the Final Panel would send the first specified aspect of Conflict A's itinerary back to the First Panel for general consideration by the entire conference.

Conflict B: Step Three

The Chinese Ambassador conducts a simple majority vote within the First Panel on the first specified aspect of Conflict B's itinerary.

Week Eight

Conflict A: Step Eight

The Venezuelan delegation submits a survey to the UN Secretary-General, who reports on Conflict A to the UN General Assembly.

Conflict B: Step Four

The Final Panel will respond to the First Panel's vote in one of two manners. It can accept the decision promulgated by the First Panel, or, it can request that the American Ambassador conduct a simple majority vote within the Final Panel, in the event of: (1) a 4–4 deadlock within the First Panel; or (2) any dissatisfaction among members of the Final Panel.

Week Nine

Conflict A: Step One/Round Two

The Chinese Ambassador opens the second round of the peace process for Conflict A. Firstly, the Chinese Ambassador presides over reports to the conference regarding: (1) the status of the peacekeeping forces; and (2) the current status of Conflict A.

Secondly, the Chinese Ambassador will accept proposals from the conference for: (1) the reconsideration of the first specified aspect, should it be returned to the First Panel; or (2) the second aspect specified on Conflict A's itinerary. (Should any specified aspect be subject to reconsideration, it will repeat the entire eight-step process.)

Conflict B: Step Five

Should the Final Panel challenge the First Panel's decision, the American Ambassador will appeal to the American Ambassador to the United Nations, who will take the issue to the UN Security Council.

Week Ten

Conflict A: Step Two/Round Two

The Chinese Ambassador leads a general discussion on the proposals for the second specified aspect of Conflict B's itinerary.

Conflict B: Step Six

The American Ambassador to the United Nations requests a vote within the fifteen-member UN Security Council. A simple majority vote of eight will do one of two things. It will uphold the decision of the First Panel, or, it will enable the Final Panel to resolve—through a simple majority vote of three—the first specified aspect of Conflict B's itinerary.

Week Eleven

Conflict A: Step Three/Round Two

The Chinese Ambassador conducts a simple majority vote within the First Panel to endorse one of the proposals on the second specified aspect of the Conflict A's itinerary.

Conflict B: Step Seven

The Final Panel will respond in one of two manners. It can accept the decision by the UN Security Council, or, it can request that the American Ambassador conduct a vote within the Final Panel to overrule the UN Security Council, should the latter uphold the First Panel's decision. A four-to-one decision by the Final Panel will send the first specified aspect of the Conflict B's itinerary back to the First Panel for a general reconsideration by the entire conference.

Week Twelve

Conflict A: Step Four/Round Two

The Final Panel will respond to the First Panel's vote in one of two manners. It can accept the decision promulgated by the First Panel, or, it can request that the American Ambassador conduct a simple majority vote within the Final Panel, in the event of: (1) a 4–4 deadlock within the First Panel; or (2) any dissatisfaction among members of the Final Panel.

Conflict B: Step Eight

The Venezuelan Ambassador submits a survey to the UN Secretary-General, who reports to the UN General Assembly on the peace process regarding Conflict B.

Week Thirteen

Conflict A: Step Five/Round Two

Should the Final Panel challenge the First Panel's decision, the American Ambassador will appeal to the U.S. Ambassador to the United Nations. In turn, the USUN Ambassador will raise the issue in the UN Security Council.

Conflict B: Step One/Round Two

The Chinese Ambassador begins the second round of the Conflict B's peace process. Firstly, the Chinese Ambassador receives a report from the special envoy assigned to mediate between the warring sides in Conflict B. Secondly, the Chinese Ambassador accepts proposals on either: (1) a complete, eight-step reconsideration of the first specified aspect; or (2) the second specified aspect of Conflict B's itinerary.

Week Fourteen

Conflict A: Step Six/Round Two

The American Ambassador to the United Nations requests a vote within the fifteen-member UN Security Council. It will uphold the decision of the First Panel, or, it will enable the Final Panel to resolve—through a simple majority vote of three—the second specific aspect on the itinerary for Conflict A.

Conflict B: Step Two/Round Two

The Chinese Ambassador leads a general discussion of the proposals for the first specified aspect on the Conflict B's itinerary.

Week Fifteen

Conflict A: Step Seven/Round Two

The Final panel will respond in one of two manners. It can accept the decision by the UN Security Council, or, it can request that the American Ambassador conduct a vote within the Final Panel to overrule the UN Security Council, should the latter uphold the First Panel's decision. A four-to-one decision by the Final Panel will send the second specified aspect on the Conflict A's itinerary back to the First Panel for a general reconsideration by the entire conference.

Conflict B: Step Three/Round Two

The Chinese Ambassador conducts a simple majority vote within the First panel on the specified aspect of Conflict B's itinerary.

Week Sixteen

Conflict A: Step Eight/Round Two

The Venezuelan Ambassador submits a survey to the UN Secretary-General, who reports to the UN General Assembly on Conflict B.

Conflict B: Step Four/Round Two

The Final Panel will respond to the First Panel's vote in one of two manners. It can accept the decision promulgated by the First Panel, or, it can request that the American Ambassador conduct a simple majority vote within the Final Panel, in the event of: (1) a 4–4 deadlock within the First Panel; or (2) any dissatisfaction among members of the Final Panel.

* * *

This proposed conference is based upon an international arms sale and transfer. Saudi Arabia is to finance the purchase of these arms. In this initiative, Israel is to sell conventional arms to the Arab Republic of Egypt. Egypt, in turn, is to provide these Israeli arms to the countries selected by, *inter alios,* Saudi Arabia, for peacekeeping duties in the regions designated. As a *quid pro quo* for its financial sponsorship, Saudi Arabia would facilitate the full participation of a Palestinian delegation comprised of representatives from not only the West Bank and Gaza, but also from: (1) East Jerusalem; and (2) the Palestinian Diaspora.

The Saudi-Egyptian-Israeli arms entente will provide the basis for the forementioned peace process, to be implemented by: (1) the thirteen conferees; and (2) a contact group, to reconcile warring factions within specific regional disputes. It seems paradoxical that an arms sale might provide the linchpin for an international peace process, but as Andrew J. Pierre, an expert in international arms sales, once wrote:

Arms sales have become, more than ever before, a crucial dimension of world politics. They are now major strands in the warp and woof of international affairs. Arms sales are far more than an economic occurrence, a military relationship, or an arms control challenge—arms sales are foreign policy writ large.[18]

As a conference cochairman, the People's Republic of China would join the United States in supervising this conventional arms transfer. Diplomatically, the PRC has formal relations with all of the key players in this transaction. The Palestine Liberation Organization formalized its diplomacy with China on 20 November 1988. Diplomatic relations between Beijing and Riyadh were established on 22 July 1990.[19] Sino-Israeli relations were formalized on 24 January 1992. And China's arms activities in the Middle East have included limited coproduction with, *inter alios,* the Arab Republic of Egypt. As explained earlier, these nations would cooperate to arm peacekeepers designated to facilitate the resolution of regional disputes.[20]

China's record on UN peacekeeping forces, however, is not one that inspires confidence. In the past Middle Eastern crises, the PRC has either withheld its endorsement or stood in outright opposition to: (1) UNEF I, the United Nations Emergency Forces, after the 1956 Suez war; (2) the United Nations Forces in Cyprus (UNFICYP), which were formed in 1965; (3) UNEF II, assigned after the October 1973 war to the Sinai Peninsula: (4) UNDOF, the United Nations Disengagement Force, also organized after the 1973 war, to patrol the Golan Heights; and (5) UNIFIL, the United Nations Interim Force in Lebanon, formed in March 1978 to monitor the civil war and Syrian-Israeli presence in that nation.[21]

It thus behooves prospective policymakers to briefly review China's attitude toward arms control, especially in the Middle East.

China and Middle Eastern Arms Control

The absence of Sino-American arms-control cooperation—in both nuclear and conventional aspects—has provided a source of continuing contention between Beijing and Washington. As Harry Harding explained:

> Although Peking was willing to conduct military exchanges with the United States and was eager to acquire American military technology, it was not prepared to coordinate its broader foreign policy with that of the United States. In the late 1980s, differences between the two countries emerged on several global and regional issues, **most notably China's arms sales to the Middle East,** its apparent violation of the norms against the proliferation of nuclear weapons and its continuing assistance to the Khmer Rouge in Cambodia.[22] (Emphasis added)

China's arms transfers to the Middle East began in 1966, in the form of assistance to the newly formed Palestine Liberation Organization. Until the Soviet-Syrian arms pipeline to the PLO began in the early 1970s, the PRC provided the most military material.[23]

China's military assistance was not limited to just the Palestine Liberation Organization. According to Yitzhak Schichor, the PRC also provided Iraq with a steady flow of arms through the 1980s. Writing in *Problems of Communism,* he explained:

> Following the eruption of the Iran-Iraq war in September 1980, Baghdad became China's leading arms customer. From 1982 to 1989, the estimated value of Chinese arms delivered to Iraq was $4.16 billion, nearly 32 percent of the value of all PRC arms deliveries in that period.[24]

The Beijing-to-Baghdad arms pipeline was closed after 2 August 1991, when Iraq invaded Kuwait. In compliance with Operative Paragraph Three, Clause (c) of United Nations Security Council Resolution 661—promulgated on 6 August 1990—China discontinued all arms deliveries to Iraq, its primary purchaser. Yitzhak Schichor qualified, however, that "other Chinese arms sales, to the Middle East and other regions, continued."[25] Lillian Craig Harris corroborated this qualification in *China Considers the Middle East:*

> By the mid-1980s, 80 percent of China's arms exports were going to the Middle East, North Africa and the Sudan, and five of China's seven best arms customers were Middle Eastern states: Iraq, Iran, Egypt, Syria and Libya. Despite the end of the Iran-Iraq war in 1988, the Middle East remained China's major arms market and cooperation extended to co-production of certain items with Egypt, Iraq, Iran and Israel.[26]

Washington has historically regarded Beijing's arms transfers to Tehran to be the most disagreeable dimension of the PRC's policy toward the Middle East. On 10 October 1986—during Defense Secretary Caspar Weinberger's visit to Beijing—the Reagan Administration announced that continued U.S. technology transfers to China would be contingent on the cessation of Chinese arms supplies to Iran. Sanctions were imposed in June 1991, after America ascertained the transfer of the Chinese M-11 missiles to Pakistan. (The M-11's technology—which was developed in China—can propel a warhead to a maximum range of three hundred miles.) The June 1991 sanctions—which were unrelated to those imposed after the 1989 Tiananmen Square massacre—effectively froze twenty pending licenses for the sale by the Commerce Department to China of $30 million in high-speed computers. The 1991 sanctions were lifted on 21 February 1992, after the Bush Administration had received a PRC pledge to forego further sales of missiles and missile technologies to the Middle East.[27]

Then, on 23 July 1993, the United States charged China with transporting chemicals to Iran that could be used in the making of chemical weapons. Specifically, America accused the Chinese cargo ship *Yin He* of carrying two chemical weapon precursors: (1) thiodiglycol, the basic ingredient of mustard gas; and (2) thionyl chloride, the basis for nerve gas.[28] This resulted in a decision—made on 25 August 1993—by the United States to ban satellite exports to Beijing. The ban affected approximately $1 billion in U.S. exports to the PRC.[29] It was to be of two years' duration, and was to be applied against: (1) two Chinese government ministries; (2) eight Chinese companies; and (3) Pakistan's Defense Ministry.[30]

PRC-Pakistani arms transactions—i.e., the sale and transfer of M-11 intermediate-range missile components in November 1992—have also drawn the opprobrium of America's intelligence agencies. And when the United States refused to sell intermediate-range missiles to Saudi Arabia—in accordance with the Intermediate Nuclear Force Agreement of December 1987—defense policymakers in Riyadh turned to China, which sold to Saudi Arabia its CSS-2 missiles. (This arms sale should be placed in the context of a broader commercial relationship. In his book, *China's Changing Relations with the Middle East,* John Calabrese wrote that "in every year from 1982 to 1986—a trend that began at the outset of the decade—the annual value of Chinese exports to Saudi Arabia surpassed $100 million, making the Saudi kingdom the PRC's leading Gulf trading partner."[31])

The Sino-Saudi sale subsequently: (1) drove Israel to expedite its efforts on the American-financed Jericho missile system; and (2) piqued Syria's interest in a prospective

21

PRC arms purchase. Lillian Craig Harris thusly explained that "in this way, China's transfer of sophisticated armaments to the Middle East influenced intra-Arab rivalry, the military balance in the Arab-Israeli conflict, and the U.S.–Israeli relationship.[32]

On 9 July 1991, in response to what Harry Harding described as "pressure for tighter controls on the conventional arms trade in the region," the five permanent members of the UN Security Council met in Paris. At this meeting, the Chinese delegation reportedly agreed on the need for more stringent controls on Middle Eastern weapons transfers. U.S. Representative Reginald Bartholomew —who was then Under Secretary of State for International Security Affairs used this two-day conference to seek the creation of rules, mechanisms, and patterns of consultation so as to harmonize arms transfers to the Middle East.[33]

On 25 September 1991—in an address to the forty-sixth session of the United Nations General Assembly in New York—PRC Foreign Minister Qian stated that "arms control in the Middle East should be linked to the regional peace process." He also used the occasion to call for "a conference on arms control in the Middle East," to "convene with the participation of all the countries concerned."[34] On 19 October 1991—after a two-day meeting at Lancaster House in London, United Kingdom—the five permanent UN Security Council members agreed to share information about their arms transactions to the Middle East. China, the United States, the United Kingdom, France and Russia provide approximately 85 percent of all arms exports to the Middle East.[35]

China attended the first session of the ACME talks that convened in Washington on 11 May 1992. Specifically, the five permanent members agreed on a mechanism for the transfer of information and had actually exchanged data regarding Middle Eastern arms transfers. The Chinese, however, decided to boycott the Moscow multilateral Middle East talks on arms control after the United States sold 150 F-16 aircraft to Taiwan. The American arms-sale announcement—made on 2 September 1992—was followed by a Chinese warning, during a meeting between U.S. Ambassador J. Stapleton Roy and PRC Deputy Foreign Minister Liu Huaqiu. It concurred with China's disagreement with the other four negotiators on which countries should be included in the prenotification arrangement. China wanted to include Turkey, but the negotiators from London, Washington, and Paris were averse to Istanbul's inclusion. In their article in *Arms Control Today,* Paul H. B. Godwin and John J. Schulz explained that this was because Turkey is a member of the North Atlantic Treaty Organization.[36]

Deputy Foreign Minister Liu's warning was substantiated on 16 September 1992, during Foreign Minister Qian Qichen's three-day visit to Israel. Foreign Minister Qian, in announcing China's withdrawal from the Moscow multilaterals, added that "China is prepared to play a role in the Middle East peace process but that this role should be one that is more impartial and more capable of incorporating the interests of all parties."[37]

That China's withdrawal disappointed the United States was clarified on 28 May 1993, during President Clinton's report to Congress:

> We are also concerned that China has withdrawn from the Middle East arms control (ACME) talks. The U.S. holds that, as a permanent member of the UN Security Council, China has a special responsibility to continue in these talks.[38]

Recent reports reflect growing consternation on Capitol Hill and within the Clinton Administration in reference to China's current arms activities with Iran, Iraq, and Pakistan. China's activities with Iran and Pakistan are missile-related; China's activity with Iraq connects to the 1991 Gulf War. On 3 July 1995, *Washington Post* correspondents David B. Ottaway and R. Jeffrey Smith cited CIA findings about the Pakistani possession of thirty complete M-11 missiles. These reports could lead Congress to compel the White House to impose a 1990 law that would (1) halt export licenses; (2) freeze government contracts; and (3) sever millions of dollars in bilateral trade with all countries involved. This potentiality has been raised by Sen. John McCain (Republican of Arizona) and Rep. Howard L. Berman (Democrat of California), two of the law's cosponsors.[39]

On 3 July 1995, *The Washington Times* reported that China had pledged to support Iraq when the economic embargo is reviewed by the UN Security Council. The report quoted Iraqi Vice President Taha Yassin Ramadan, who was returning home through Amman, Jordan, after visiting Vietnam and China. Specifically, the Iraqi Vice President cited a PRC pledge to implement Article 22 of Resolution 68 so as to lift or ease existing economic sanctions. United Nations Security Council Resolution 687—adopted on 3 April 1991—is a thirty-four-paragraph document. Article 22 outlines the prerequisites for the removal of "prohibitions against the import of commodities and products originating in Iraq and the prohibitions against financial transactions related thereto."[40]

Nor has China's cooperation been evident on nuclear arms control. On 16 May 1995, *The New York Times* reported that China had exploded an underground nuclear bomb at its test range in Lop Nur. This detonation—which drew criticism from Australia, Japan, and Kazakhstan—came as other nuclear weapons states are observing a moratorium.[41]

China's self-perception in the international arena, however, emerged during the negotiations leading to the renewal of the Nuclear Nonproliferation Treaty (NPT). Since becoming an NPT signatory in March of 1992, the PRC's policy has become differentiated from that of the other four permanent members of the UN Security Council.[42] On 19 April 1995, *New York Times* correspondent Barbara Crossette reported that China had publicly broken ranks with the other four nuclear-weapons powers—and permanent UN Security Council members—over the terms of an extension of the treaty. (This treaty came into force in 1970, and was renewed in May of this year.)

China was prepared to support either: (1) an extension of the treaty for an indefinite period; or (2) a series of fixed periods of no less than twenty-five years' duration. In contrast, the other four nuclear-weapons powers—i.e., Russia, France, Britain, and the United States—advocated an indefinite and unconditional extension of the Treaty on the Nonproliferation of Nuclear Weapons. Developing countries, such as Venezuela and Egypt—along with such signatories as Mexico and Indonesia—did not support an indefinite extension. China apparently prefers a status of liaison, between the industrialized West and the developing nations.[43]

Irrespective of the NPT conference's denouement, this observation reveals the PRC's perception of its role in the international community. The proposed peace conference and its structure detailed earlier will allow China to assume this responsibility. The suitability of its seating arrangement is suggested by Harry Harding in his exhaustive Sino-American history, *A Fragile Relationship:*

Moreover, although it is not a global superpower, China has great influence outside Asia. Primarily through participation in the international arms market, Peking has been able to develop diplomatic leverage in the Middle East. **As a large developing country, not closely linked with the United States, China can claim common identity with much of the third world. And as a permanent member of the United Nations Security Council, Peking is guaranteed a place in deliberations of major international issues, as well as a veto over the council's decisions."**[44] (Emphasis added)

As indicated by the second seating schematic, the two key conferees on the First Panel will be Israel and the Palestine Liberation Organization. The nations selected by the author to sit on the First Panel have been chosen for geopolitical and macroeconomic reasons. However, these nations—as well as those on the Final Panel—can be substituted in response to unforeseen disputes or crises. The inclusion of Israel and the PLO, however, is pivotal to the conference and critical to the success of its deliberations. It might thus be best that the Middle East provide the point whence to begin a brief review of China's attitudes toward the conference's developing countries.

AN UNDESIGNATED CONFERENCE CONFIGURATION

THE CHINESE AMBASSADOR

The First Panel
——*P.L.O. Israel*——

THE AMERICAN AMBASSADOR

The Final Panel
China   France   Russia   United Kingdom   United States.

Chinese Diplomacy toward the Arab-Israeli Dispute

In *China Considers the Middle East,* it was explained that "two remarkable events occurred virtually simultaneously in the late 1970s: official Chinese recognition of Israel's right to exist and China's first statements of public support for establishment of a state called 'Palestine.' "[45] Until that time—i.e., the consummation of the Egyptian-Israeli peace treaty of 25 April 1979—the paths pursued by the PRC toward the Arab and Israeli camps had not been completely dissimilar.

China's ties with Judaism antedates the Northern Sung dynasty, which existed from 960–1125 A.D. The most prominent Jewish community at that time was in the capital city of Kaifeng, which was located in what is now the Henan Province. Kaifeng, a city of 500,000, is currently campaigning to attract foreign investment from the overseas Jewish business community. Toward this end, the city has approved a "Special Economic Development Zone for Overseas Jews."[46]

British and American pressure on Dr. Sun Yat-sen induced the Republic of China to recognize: (1) the Zionist concept embodied in the Balfour Declaration of 1917; and (2) the state of Israel, in 1948. In a similar vein, Cold War pressures from the Soviet Union and the West prevented formal diplomacy from blossoming between the new nations of Israel and the People's Republic of China.[47]

European exclusionary pressure on China vis-à-vis the Middle East is not unique to the twentieth century. It was also evident in the late 1800s, as Russia competed with Great Britain for control of, access to, and influence in India. Lillian Craig Harris wrote that although "Chinese authority over Tibet, Qinghai and Xinjiang in the late nineteenth and early twentieth centuries established China as a major 'Muslim' state, China was the weakest player in the 'Great Games.' " Dr. Harris continued:

> China's Central Asian ambitions were also caught between Russia and those of British India. The south-east frontier of Tajikistan was determined in 1895 by Britain and Russia without Chinese acquiescence, and Russian and British spheres of interest in Central Asia served further to separate China from the Middle East.[48]

During the Ch'ing dynasty—from 1644 to 1912—China's Muslim population comprised 10 to 15 million of a total population approximating 125 million. In 1939—reportedly through Chinese initiative—formal ties were forged with Saudi Arabia. At that time, a consulate was opened in Jidda. As of 1992, the total of Chinese Muslims residing in Saudi Arabia were estimated at 1,000 Hui and 8 to 10,000 Uighur.[49]

Another Chinese initiative, this time toward Iran, culminated in a 1942 bilateral friendship treaty. Also established in 1942 were Republican China's relations with Egypt; relations with Lebanon and Syria were subsequently realized, two years thereafter.[50]

Within the context of the Arab-Israeli dispute that would burn through the post–World War II period, Beijing's policymakers steadfastly supported most Arab arguments. In July 1968—at the fourth session of the Palestine National Council—China's was the only non-Arab delegation in attendance.[51] And after the October 1973 war, China supported the Arab oil embargo extending into the year that followed. China also held Israel responsible for initiating that war:

After the October 1973 war, China refused to participate in two Security Council ceasefire resolutions, declaring that Israel had initiated the war and therefore it alone should be condemned. In keeping with then-majority Palestinian opinion, China rejected UNSC resolution 242 of 1967 and abstained from voting on SCR 338 of 1973 on the grounds that the resolutions sought to reduce the Palestine issue to "a refugee question" which "could be written off by the offer of a sum of compensation." This sort of UN posturing, in China's view, "neither denounces Israel's aggression nor provides for the safeguarding of the legitimate rights of the Palestinian people."[52]

This policy continued through the remainder of the 1970s and the 1980s. In January 1977, the *Peking Review* is said to have approved of the joint Egyptian-Syrian communiqué calling for a Geneva conference in which the PLO could participate on an equal footing with the other conferees. Policymakers in Beijing backed Lebanese President Amin Gemayel when he called in November 1982 for the complete withdrawal of all foreign troops from Lebanon. There is evidence that the Chinese supported a direct dialogue between the PLO and the United States. And the PRC also was said to have endorsed the endeavor—agreed upon in February 1985 by the PLO and Jordan—to coordinate a joint negotiating position to present at a future international peace conference.[53]

China's support toward inter-Arab and Arab-African disputes, however, has been more qualified and conditional. Two respective examples are the Iraqi-Kuwaiti border dispute and the Libyan invasion of Chad. PRC policies within the Arab world—just as its attitude toward arms control in the Middle East—must be viewed within the framework of its competition with the Republic of China (Taiwan).

China and the Iraqi-Kuwaiti Question

Sino-Iraqi relations were established in 1958, and began to intensify in the late 1970s. Yitzhak Schichor wrote that "by the summer of 1990, Iraq had become China's most important market for labor services and contracted projects." From 1976 to 1987, China provided Iraq with: (1) $678 million in labor exports; (2) construction services, the value of which were estimated to have exceeded $1 billion.[54]

This friendship, however, disallowed direct diplomacy with Kuwait, whose June 1961 independence led to formal relations with the ROC (Republic of China) on 22 November 1963. The logic underpinning this disallowance was explained by Yitzhak Schichor:

> . . . the Chinese were caught in a difficult dilemma. On the one hand, they wanted to recognize the independence of Kuwait. Yet, on the other hand, they realized that recognition of Kuwait's independence would upset China's already delicate relations with Iraq, which, three years earlier, had become the fourth Middle Eastern government to establish diplomatic relations with the People's Republic of China (PRC). The Iraqi ambassador to Beijing left no room for doubt on this score. In unequivocal terms, he warned the PRC that "Kuwait is a part of the Republic of Iraq, just as Taiwan is a part of China . . . "[55]

The PRC did not establish a presence in Kuwait until 1966, when Xinhua opened an office there. It was not until ten years after Kuwait's declaration of independence—on 22 March 1971—that the People's Republic of China was able to open official relations with Kuwait. Concomitant with this development was a severance of Kuwaiti ties to the ROC on Taiwan. Thereafter, Kuwait became a channel for re-exports to other parts of the Arabian Peninsula. It also became China's second most important market—after Iraq—for construction projects and labor services.[56]

By maintaining relations with both Kuwait and Iraq, China expanded economic ties to the entire Gulf region. By 1985, China's projects in the Gulf region equalled an estimated $600 million. Between 1979 and 1986, approximately 20,000 Chinese workers were in Iraq; their efforts were directed toward the completion of more than 140 projects. Conversely, the Kuwait Fund for Arab Economic Development provided China with $310 million to finance the construction of 134 projects and several joint ventures. (Joint Sino-Arab ventures—a PRC priority—numbered only twelve by 1990.) This cooperation—extending from 1982 to 1989—was remarkable in that Kuwait was the only developing nation to provide the PRC with loans. Its economic assistance, moreover, was not contingent upon an adjustment of China's domestic (i.e., human rights) policies.[57]

In the immediate prewar period, the PRC's trade volume with the Gulf exceeded $2 billion. The total number of Sino-Arab labor contracts consummated between the late 1970s and 1990 were said to number 1,900, and were valued at $3 billion. Specifically, China was estimated to have signed $1.9 billion in labor-service contracts with Iraq and $500 million in labor-service contracts with Kuwait. The ten thousand Chinese laborers who diligently worked in the Gulf nations are reported to have increased the PRC's prestige and stature in the region.[58]

The Iraqi invasion of Kuwait (on 2 August 1990) drew different reactions from foreign-policy strategists in Taipei and Beijing. Because Kuwait was then Taiwan's second-largest supplier of oil, the ROC response was more macroeconomic in orientation. Specifically, Taipei channeled its funds—through its International Economic Cooperation and Development Fund—to Jordan, Egypt, and Turkey. It also opened a new Taipei Economic and Cultural Representative Office in Riyadh, to replace the ROC Embassy that was closed in July 1990 following the establishment of Sino-Saudi diplomatic relations. (Saudi Arabia and China established full diplomatic relations on 22 July 1990.)[59]

In contrast, the PRC preoccupied itself with the geopolitical ramifications of the invasion. Specifically, China abstained from voting on UN Security Council Resolution 678 when it was tabled on 29 November 1990. Resolution 678 passed by a 12–21 vote, with Yemen and Cuba opposing the use of force. Operative Paragraph Two of this resolution authorized "Member States cooperating with the Government of Kuwait" to respond militarily to drive Iraq out of Kuwait so as "to restore international peace and security in the area," if President Hussein did not withdraw his forces by 15 January 1991. As Lillian Craig Harris explained:

> Arab dissatisfaction with China was inevitable, for Iraq and the Palestinians wanted a Chinese veto while the moderate Arabs sought Chinese consent. In the end China gave neither.[60]

Sino-Arab differences date to the early 1980s, during Libya's military occupation of the Aouzou Strip in northern Chad. After imploring Libya to respect the decisions of the Organization of African Unity, China urged a peaceful resolution of the conflict.[61]

China and the First Panel

As do most countries, China regards Egypt—and its

president, Gamal Abdel Nasser—as the traditional leader of the Arab League and the Organization of African Unity. This was clarified in December 1982, during Premier Zhao Ziyang's visit to Cairo at the start of an eleven-nation African tour. This visit, the first by a Chinese premier since Chou En-lai's final trip to Egypt in December 1963, is said to have reaffirmed China's acknowledgment of Egypt's pre-eminent stature on Arab and African affairs. In his book, *China's Changing Relations with the Middle East,* John Calabrese explained that the motivations impelling the 1963 and 1982 visits were identical:

> In December 1982 Zhao Ziyang became the first Chinese Premier to visit Cairo in nineteen years. Like his predecessor, Zhao sought to solidify Sino-Egyptian relations in order to enhance China's position, not only in the Middle East but through the Third World. Following the collapse of Sino-Soviet entente Chou En-lai in 1963 had sought to rehabilitate China's image as an independent actor, depending on Egypt to serve, among other things, as a bridgehead to Africa. Similarly, Zhao, nearly two decades later, used Cairo as the jumping-off point for an eleven-nation tour of Africa which aimed at restoring China's standing within the Nonaligned Movement following several years of Sino-American alignment. Thus, with the March 1983 New Delhi conference of nonaligned nations looming on the horizon, Zhao's visit to Egypt launched a broad Chinese campaign to regain the confidence of the Third World.[62]

Sino-Egyptian relations were established on 16 May 1956, with Cairo serving as China's first embassy in Africa. Diplomatic normalization had been preceded by two commercial agreements: (1) an August 1955 bilateral agreement favoring the Egyptian cotton industry; and (2) a Chinese liaison, also in 1955, facilitating an arms accord between Egypt and Czechoslovakia.[63]

China is thus likely to embrace a First Panel of southern hemispheric nations that includes Egypt, and Egypt is likely to endorse the two-tier arms-control mechanism that propels the forementioned conference. This was suggested on 11 June 1995 when in a *Newsweek* interview that was reprinted in *The Washington Post,* Egyptian President Hosni Mubarak explained to columnist Lally Weymouth about the need to induce Israel and the PLO toward compromise.[64]

Since his first visit to Africa in 1990, Foreign Minister Qian Qichen has visited more than twenty African nations.[65] China's chief diplomat therefore realizes that within sub-Saharan Africa and beyond, South Africa has emerged as both a diplomatic and commercial force. In his address to the UN General Assembly on 28 September 1994, PRC Foreign Minister Qian Qichen made this clear:

> I wish to avail myself of this opportunity to extend hearty welcome and congratulations to the delegation of South Africa taking part in the work of the current session. We are convinced that a united, democratic and non-racial new South Africa led by President Nelson Mandela will contribute positively to the peace and development of Africa and the world as a whole.[66]

Also on the First Panel will be four conferees from Latin America. PRC policy toward Latin America, as all aspects of Chinese diplomacy, must be examined through the prism of PRC-ROC competition. While mainland China enjoys official relations with most major Latin nations, Taiwan has managed to maintain ties with seven, mostly Central American and Caribbean nations. Through the initiative of ROC Foreign Minister Frederick F. Chien, these Latin nations have endorsed Taiwan's efforts to return to the United Nations General Assembly. Taiwan has been excluded from the UN since 1971, when mainland China assumed its permanent position on the Security Council.[67]

China and the Final Panel

Were the leadership in Beijing to reject this conference co-chairmanship initiative as an insufficient reason to adopt a more flexible human rights policy, policymakers in Washington could consider the prospect of substituting Taiwan or Japan on the Final Panel. The possible substitution of China by either of its two Asian rivals in the Middle East might provide an added incentive for Chinese cooperation.[68]

Were Taiwan to realize its aspiration of winning a seat in the United Nations General Assembly, it would first need to perform in a public forum in which it could openly demonstrate its abilities to the international community. The leadership in Taipei—which in 1991 hosted the first Arab-Chinese Conference on Systems and Technology of Information—would quickly seize this opportunity to burnish its international image.[69] By attending the forementioned conference in mainland China's stead, the ROC could "create a place in international affairs for Taiwan that would be commensurate with its growing economic clout." (Please refer to the alternative seating configuration on the following page.) As explained in *A Fragile Relationship:*

In response to these demands, the Kuomintang unveiled a policy known as flexible diplomacy, under which Taiwan would, as possible, establish formal diplomatic ties with nations that simultaneously recognized Peking as well as

Taipei, build unofficial economic and commercial links with Communist nations in Europe and Asia, upgrade unofficial ties with nations with which it could not establish diplomatic relations, and **rejoin international organizations under such names as "Chinese Taipei" or "Taipei, China."** This policy of flexible diplomacy alarmed Peking even more than the calls for self-determination, since it was sponsored by the ruling party on Taiwan.[70] (Emphasis added)

A FULLY-DESIGNATED CONFERENCE CONFIGURATION

THE CHINESE AMBASSADOR

The First Panel
Argentina Venezuela South Africa P.L.O. Israel Egypt Cuba Brazil

THE AMERICAN AMBASSADOR

The Final Panel
R.O.C. France Russia United Kingdom United States

The potentiality of a Japanese replacement of China—coupled with a concomitant replacement of Russia by Germany—would compel policymakers in Beijing to carefully consider the consequences of a continued obstinance in its attitudes on human rights. That the PRC is averse to increased Japanese diplomatic and military influence in the Middle East was evident during the 1991 Gulf War. It was also evident on 28 and 29 January 1992, during the two-day multilateral negotiations that transpired in Moscow.

The Moscow multilaterals followed the Madrid Conference for Middle East Peace, which convened from 30 October to 1 November 1991. The Moscow multilateral conferees included China, Japan, Turkey, the European

36

Community, Saudi Arabia, and other Arab Gulf countries. At this meeting, a decision was reached to establish five small working groups, each of which would address a specific problem of the Middle East, to convene in capitals in April and May across the globe. Economic-development talks were to begin in Belgium; environmental negotiations were to take place in Tokyo; arms-control and regional-security negotiations would occur in Washington, refugee-elated deliberaitons would occur in Ottawa; and water-resource questions would be addressed in Austria or Turkey.[71] Lillian Craig Harris explained that the possible recurrence of China's marginalization in the Middle East deliberations was a primary preoccupation of PRC's geopolitical strategists:

> . . . although the opening of the peace conference virtually guaranteed the establishment of Chinese ties with Israel, it did not guarantee a major role for China in the conference. China knew that its foreign minister would be only one among nearly 40 at the multilateral stage of the peace conference in Moscow. But it was vital to be there in the early stages while subjects for future discussion, and spheres of influence within them, were mapped out. **The prospect that Japan, backed by the United States, might host one of the projected multilateral working groups on Middle East problems added urgency.**[72] (Emphasis added)

The concept of a five-member Final Panel, including two nonnuclear states, Germany and Japan, both of whom aspire to permanent seats on the UN Security Council, would certainly win strong support among developing, nonnuclear nations. (Please refer to the seating configuration on the following page.) Efficient and professional performances by Germany and Japan during the conference

37

could capture the imaginations of UN reformers and would also advance their ambitions for permanent positions on the Security Council. This potentiality was addressed by Secretary of State Warren Christopher, in an address to the National Press Club in Washington, D.C., on 28 July 1995. At that time, Secretary Christopher outlined President Clinton's current policy toward Asia in an address entitled "U.S. National Interest in the Asia-Pacific Region":

A FULLY-DESIGNATED CONFERENCE CONFIGURATION

THE JAPANESE AMBASSADOR

The First Panel
Argentina Venezuela South Africa P.L.O. Israel Egypt Cuba Brazil

THE GERMAN AMBASSADOR

The Final Panel
Japan France United States United Kingdom Germany

In the post cold war world, we feel that Japan is in a position to take on even greater responsibilities than in the past, and that is why **we are supporting Japan's bid to become a permanent member of the U.N. Security Council.** Together we are doing a number of important things already. For example, supporting reform in Russia, peace in the Middle East, and stability in Haiti. And together we are addressing complex global issues like unsustainable population growth, AIDS and pollution through what we call our common agenda. And so, working together, what we have done, makes us feel that Japan can even do more to take its place as one of the great countries in the world.[73] (Emphasis added)

To forestall this development, Russia would certainly

pressure China to demonstrate greater compassion in its human-rights deliberations. The two nuclear powers have recently repaired relations, as a reflection of the shared Sino-Russian resentment toward American admonitions on their respective human-rights policies.[74]

This approach could also win U.S. Senatorial support. In his Senate statement of 18 May 1994, Sen. Bill Bradley made the following observation:

> For our credibility and impact, we must eliminate the appearance that human rights is only a bizarre American preoccupation and actively seek out ways to exert concerted Asian and international pressure on Beijing.[75]

The forementioned Middle East arms-control negotiations notwithstanding, China's cooperation with the four other permanent members of the UN Security Council has heretofore been focused primarily upon Asia. Since 1980, areas of cooperation have included: (1) the enhancement of security on the Korean peninsula; (2) the implementation of the Paris peace accords in Cambodia; (3) the Soviet withdrawal from Afghanistan; and (4) the encouragement of peaceful coexistence between India and Pakistan.[76]

China, however, has heretofore been excluded from contributing to the deliberations and diplomacy regarding the Wars of Yugoslav Succession. Peace efforts in Bosnia—conducted by the United States, Germany, France, Britain, and Russia—have reached an impasse. Paradoxically, it is in the former Yugoslavia where Russia and the West could employ China's experience in Eastern Europe to its most positive end. This was explained by Dr. David Zweig, a professor at the Fletcher School of Law and Diplomacy:

... the United States needs Chinese support for resolving many global crises, **including the war in Yugoslavia** ... With its seat in the United Nations, China has a great deal of power over the UN's development into a multilateral peacekeeping force and over the Security Council's ability to become a real center for negotiating solutions to crises.[77] (Emphasis added)

Sino-Yugoslav relations antedate 4 October 1949, when Josip Broz Tito's overture for recognition of the nascent PRC was ignored by Mao Zedong. Bilateral relations between these Cominform members were established in January 1955. Relations were severed from 1958 to 1970 and were resumed largely as a result of shared opposition to the Soviet invasion of Czechoslovakia in 1968.[78]

Were the Chinese cochairman to place the Bosnian question on the agenda of the proposed conference—perhaps with direct German mediation between the Croats, Serbs, and Muslims—it is likely that European endorsement would quickly follow. On 1 February 1995, French Foreign Minister Alain Juppé proposed a meeting of Bosnian, Serbian, and Croatian leaders and a new international conference to try to break the deadlock on a peace settlement for Bosnia. The proposal—which was broached in an article published in *Le Monde* on 31 January 1995 and summarized in an article appearing in *The New York Times* on 1 February 1995—has been endorsed by German Foreign Minister Klaus Kinkel.[79]

The French are likely to favor any proposal that can facilitate: (1) a joint delegation of representatives from the Republic of China and the People's Republic of China; and thusly, (2) a direct meeting between the leaders of Taiwan and the Chinese mainland. The conundrum of cross-strait politics was squarely addressed by Mr. Jacques Friedmann, a special envoy of then French Prime Minister Edouard Balladur. Mr. Friedmann, who visited Beijing from 23 to 28 December 1993, met with Premier Li Peng, Foreign Minister and Vice Premier Qian Qichen and Vice Foreign Minister Jiang Enzhu. These deliberations produced a brief bilateral communiqué, an excerpt of which follows:

> The Chinese side has reaffirmed its consistent position on the question of Taiwan. The French side has confirmed that the French Government recognizes the Government of the People's Republic of China as the sole legal government of China and Taiwan as an integral part of Chinese territory.[80]

A proposal promoting Sino-Western entente was recently requested by the European Union. (EU-Chinese bilateral diplomatic relations were established in 1975 and expanded in 1985, through a Trade and Cooperation Agreement). On 5 July 1995, Sir Leon Brittan called on both the U.S. and the PRC to show more flexibility in their bilateral discussions. Mr. Brittan—who is the European Union's trade commissioner—outlined the European Commission's new strategy on relations with China. Speaking in Brussels, he explained that Europe should endeavor to bring China into the international political and economic system:

> The aim now is to place the full breadth of Europe's ties with China within a single strategic framework which will be flexible enough to deal with unforeseen events but ambitious enough to take advantage of the continued rise in China's importance over the coming years. . . . I am convinced that it is in Europe's vital interest to steer China into the world economic and political mainstream and away from isolation. Europe must continue to push for China's full participation in the international community, for this

will help cement reform within China itself as well as making China a source of stability in Asia and beyond.[81]

Recent remarks indicate that an international conference that facilitates a direct meeting between ROC and PRC chiefs-of-state is certain to attract policymakers in Taipei and Beijing. On 30 January 1995—at a tea part in Beijing's Great Hall of the People—Pres. Jiang Zemin delivered a speech titled "Continue to Promote the Reunification of the Motherland." The PRC President and the CCP (Chinese Communist Party) General Secretary outlined eight points, the realization of which would eventually lead to reunification. In Point Three, he observed:

> We have proposed time and again that negotiations should be held on officially ending the state of hostility between the two sides and accomplishing peaceful reunification step by step. **As regards the name, place and form of these political talks, a solution acceptable to both sides can certainly be found so long as consultations on an equal footing can be held at an early date.**[82] (Emphasis added)

Taiwan's reply came two months later. On 8 April 1995, in a speech to the National Unification Council in Taipei, Taiwan President Lee Teng-hui presented a six-point plan toward the unification of Taiwan with the Chinese mainland. Point Four of the plan was titled the "Two Sides Join International Organizations on Equal Footing and Leaders of the Two Sides Will Naturally Meet Each Other on Such Occasions." So germane is Point Four of President Lee's plan—to the proposed peace conference put forth earlier in this treatise—that an excerpt is cited below.

I have repeated many times that natural meetings of leaders from the two sides on international occasions will

ease political confrontation between the two sides and foster an atmosphere of harmonious contacts and meetings. . . . This will also show the world that the Chinese people on the two sides, despite political differences, can still join hands to make contributions to the international community and create a new age for the Chinese nation to stand proud in the word.[83] (Emphasis added)

On 9 April 1995, Presidential Secretary General Wu Poh-hsiung added that the ROC government would not rule out arranging a meeting between the two leaders at a third location.

These attitudes were most recently reaffirmed by Pres. Lee Teng-hui, during his recent six-day visit to the United States. Dr. Lee's visit climaxed with a return to his alma mater, Cornell University. During his lecture to more than four thousand graduates and guests, President Lee offered to meet with CCP leader Jiang Zemin:

To demonstrate our sincerity and goodwill, I have already indicated on other occasions that I would welcome an opportunity for leaders from the mainland to meet their counterparts from Taiwan during the occasion of some international event, and I would not even rule out the possibility of a meeting between Mr. Jiang Zemin and myself.[84]

The seating arrangement offered by the proposed conference is certain to attract Chinese policymakers. On 18 January 1995—during a visit to Beijing by former Secretary of State Henry A. Kissinger—Pres. Jiang Zemin expressed the need for initiatives that promote mutual respect:

First, the two countries should build up equality. We should take great foresight and seek common ground to let Sino-

U.S. ties develop in a new pattern. This is not only in the immediate interests of the two nations, but also is aimed at the world's overall situation and its future.[85]

In his article "Clinton and China: Creating a Policy Agenda That Works," Dr. Zweig explained that "China is thus highly sensitive about its international stature and strongly wants to take what it sees as its rightful place near the top of the community of nations." And Gerald Segal, writing in *China in the Nineties,* added that "China's main focus of attention seem[s] to be in establishing itself as the champion of the South against the North."[86] In *A Fragile Relationship,* Harry Harding offers a prescription that concurs with the preceding assessments and bodes well for a Sino-American conference co-chairmanship:

> . . . the relationship between China and the United States will contain elements of cooperation and competition in almost every dimension. Rather than portraying Sino-American relations as a pure convergence or a complete divergence of interests, as was often the case in the past, it will be wiser to portray them as a mixture of complementary and competitive objectives. **Such a relationship will be primarily characterized not by antagonism, nor by harmony, but rather by hard bargaining with complicated trade-offs within and between issues.**[87] (Emphasis added)

Historically, however, most Sino-American cooperation toward regional disputes—e.g., coordinated conventional arms transfers to resistance fighters serving in the Afghan *mujahedin*—has been coordinated in response to Soviet aggression, within the context of Cold War geopolitics. Harry Harding wrote that China had even "expressed support for an American military presence abroad, as long as it could be justified as part of a strategy to contain Soviet hegemonism.[88] In concurrence, Lillian Craig Harris wrote:

> The Middle East has been a major source of tension between China and the United States since establishment of official Sino-U.S. relations in 1979. **Rarely has China coordinated its policy with that of the United States, and then only under the duress of feared Soviet gain,** as after the Soviet invasion of Afghanistan in 1979, or through the need to conform to international consensus as during the 1990–91 Gulf crisis.[89] (Emphasis added)

This initiative attempts to base U.S.-PRC relations upon a more positive premise. It is based on a reality recognized, *inter alios,* by Joan E. Spero, the U.S. Under Secretary of State for Economic and Agricultural Affairs. On 25 February 1994—in an address before the Congressional International Economic Issues Forum, Washington, D.C.—she explained that "the Cold War is over, and with it has gone our traditional frame of reference for looking at our international involvement."[90]

The proposed conference does not attempt to "contain" Russia or any other nation, but instead endeavors toward cooperation among allies and former cold-war competitors to construct governments of national unity where regional disputes now exist. This endeavor is based upon the Camp David Peace Accords of 17 September 1978, the Egyptian-Israeli peace treaty of 25 April 1979, and the PLO-Israeli Declaration of Principles of 13 September 1993. It was constructed to promote the policy of engagement recently articulated by Secretary of State Christopher:

> The policy of engagement reflects the fundamental understanding that our ability to pursue significant common interests and to manage significant disinterest, would not

be served by any attempt to isolate or contain China. We do not intend to try to do so. The wisdom of this historic judgment of engagement has demonstrated time and again that our ability to work together on key challenges of regional and global importance will be best manifested by being engaged.[91]

As mentioned earlier, this conference could facilitate cooperation and a direct dialogue between Taiwan and the continental China. Only once—in Singapore, from 27 to 29 April 1993—did ROC and PRC representatives meet directly. That meeting produced four agreements that serve as interim steps toward the normalization of cross-Strait relations.[92]

Because of President Lee's six-day visit to the United States, the PRC postponed the second round of its talks with Taiwan. The PRC-ROC bilaterals, which were projected to transpire in the middle of July, were to have been conducted by: (1) Wang Dao-han, chairman of the PRC Association for Relations Across the Taiwan Straits; and (2) Koo Chen-fu, chairman of the ROC Straits Exchange Foundation.[93]

On 12 July 1995, China underscored its displeasure by asking the United States to pledge that: (1) Taiwan is a part of China; and (2) Taiwan President Lee would not be allowed to make any more visits to the United States. This request was reinforced on 21 and 22 July 1995, when China fired four test missiles off Taiwan's southern coast.[94]

This initiative could indirectly facilitate a meaningful resumption of the PRC-ROC dialogue. The desirability of such a dialogue was clarified by Secretary of State Christopher on 28 July 1995, in his address to the National Press Club in Washington, D.C.:

We think that there is no basis for threats between the parties. As a matter of fact, one of things I'd like to emphasize here today is the importance of China and Taiwan working out the problems together. There have been discussions between them. Those discussions should continue. That's the way to resolve those problems, in dialogue and in peace.[95]

For this proposed conference to convene, however, there must beforehand be a fundamental improvement in relations between the People's Republic of China and the United States of America. Indeed, it was the lack of concurrence on Sino-American issues of contention that, *inter alia*, precluded the PRC from participating in the Madrid Conference from 30 October to 4 November 1991. As Lillian Craig Harris explained:

That China expressed willingness to attend the peace conference and was not invited to do so constituted a rebuff. However, **in addition to the Israeli barrier, China faced American disfavour over its arms sales policy, human rights record, and evasion of American tariff and copyright regulations.** To save face and to maintain an appearance of international significance in keeping with its Security Council position, China had to move carefully. Failure to get to the conference would deal a crippling blow to China's image as champion of Palestinian and other developing world causes. In Cairo, a Xinhua journalist worried privately that prospects for China's international activism more generally would be damaged if China were locked out of the Middle East conference.[96] (Emphasis added)

China's attitude toward the control, sale, and transfer of arms has already been briefly reviewed, as has the proposed conference which could prospectively be offered

47

by American policymakers. The following pages will attempt to chronicle the Clinton Administration's endeavors toward the improvement of PRC policies on trade, intellectual property, and human rights. It endeavors to provide background material for the foreign-policy novice, and a reference tool for the professional policymaker.

Notes

1. Harry Harding, *A Fragile Relationship: The United States and China since 1972* (Washington, D.C.: The Brookings Institution, 1992), p. 332.
2. Lillian Craig Harris, *China Considers the Middle East* (London and New York: I. B. Tauris & Co. Ltd., 1993), p. 20.
3. Senator Bill Bradley, "Floor Statement by Senator Bill Bradley on China's Most Favored Nation Status," 18 May 1994, pp. 2, 3.
4. Thomas W. Lippman, "Envoys Offer Evidence of Waning U.S. Muscle," *Washington Post*, 28 May 1995, p. A-37.
5. John Shattuck, "Human Rights and Democracy in Asia: Address to the Asia Foundations' Center for Asian Pacific Affairs, Alexandria, Virginia, June 28, 1994," *U.S. Department of State Dispatch*, 18 July 1994, Vol. 5, No. 29, p. 482.
6. Warren Christopher, "U.S. National Interest in the Asia-Pacific Region," Address by the Secretary of State to the National Press Club, Washington, D.C., 28 July 1995, p. 10.
7. Lillian Craig Harris, op. cit., pp. 183, 184.
8. Harris, op. cit., pp. 196, 197.
9. "UNGA Resolution 36/120C," 10 December 1981, *Resolutions and Decisions Adopted by the General Assembly during Its Thirty-sixth Session*, Supplement No. 51 (A/36/51), (New York: United Nations, 1982), p. 27.
10. Harris, op. cit., pp. 183–85.
11. Harris, op. cit., pp. 185, 186, 240.
12. Ibid., pp. 185, 186.
13. "Arafat's Beijing Speech," *FBIS-China*, 10 October 1989, p. 13.
14. Harris, op. cit., p. 264; "Qian Qichen Addresses UN General Assembly," *FBIS-China*, 26 September 1991, p. 6.

15. "No Plans for South Africa, Israel Ties," *FBIS-China*, 26 September 1991, p. 2.
16. Harris, op. cit., p. 262.
17. Ibid., p. 263; Sheryl WuDunn, "Israel Agrees to Ties with China, Aiding Beijing Role in Talks," *New York Times*, 24 January 1992, p. A–9.
18. Andrew J. Pierre, "Arms Sales: The New Diplomacy," *Foreign Affairs*, Vol. 60, No. 2 (Winter 1981/82), pp. 266–86.
19. "Recognition from China," *New York Times*, 21 November 1988, p. A–11; "Riyadh and Beijing Declare Start of Full Diplomatic Ties," *New York Times*, 22 July 1990, p. I–6.
20. Yitzhak Schichor, "China and the Gulf Crisis: Escape from Predicaments," *Problems of Communism*, Vol. XL, No. 6 (November–December 1991), p. 89; Harris, op. cit., p. 259.
21. Harris, op. cit., pp. 131, 132.
22. Harding, op. cit., p. 15.
23. Harris, op. cit., pp. 161, 162.
24. Schichor, op. cit., p. 82.
25. "Resolution 661 of 6 August 1990," *Resolutions and Decisions of the Security Council: 1990*, Document S/INF/46, (New York: United Nations, 1991), pp. 19, 20; and Schichor, op. cit., p. 84.
26. Harris, op. cit., pp. 200, 246.
27. Harris, op. cit., p. 193; Elaine Sciolino, "U.S. Lifts Its Sanctions on China over High-Technology Transfers," *New York Times*, 22 February 1992, p. 1; Steven Greenhouse, "$1 Billion in Sales of High-Tech Items to China Blocked," *New York Times*, 26 August 1993, p. A–15.
28. Li Daoyu, "Foreign Policy and Arms Control: The View from China," *Arms Control Today*, Vol. 23, No. 10 (December 1993), p. 10; and Nicholas D. Kristof, "China Says U.S. Is Harassing Ship Suspected of Taking Arms to Iran," *New York Times*, 9 August 1993, p. A–6.
29. Joseph Fewsmith, "America and China: Back from the Brink," *Current History*, Vol. 93, No. 584 (September 1994), p. 252; *The Economist*, 5 November 1994, p. 67; Steven Greenhouse, "$1 Billion in Sales of High-Tech Items to China Blocked," *New York Times*, 26 August 1993, p. A–1.
30. Paul H. B. Godwin and John J. Schulz, "China and Arms Control: Transition in East Asia," *Arms Control Today*, Vol. 24, No. 9 (November 1994), p. 11.

31. John Calabrese, *China's Changing Relations with the Middle East* (London and New York: Pinter Publishers, 1991), p. 148.

32. Fewsmith, op. cit., p. 252; Harris, op. cit., p. 193; William J. Clinton, "Report to Congress Concerning Extension of Waiver Authority for the People's Republic of China," 28 May 1993, *Public Papers of the Presidents of the United States* (Washington: U.S. Government Printing Office, 1993), p. 774.

33. Alan Riding, "5 Powers Will Seek Ban on Major Mideast Arms," *New York Times,* 10 July 1991, p. A–9.

34. "Qian Qichen Addresses UN General Assembly," *FBIS-China,* 26 September 1991, p. 5.

35. Craig R. Whitney, "U.S. and 4 Other Big Arms Makers Adopt Guidelines on Sales," *New York Times,* 20 October 1991, p. 11.

36. Paul H. B. Godwin and John J. Schulz, "China and Arms Control: Transition in East Asia," *Arms Control Today,* Vol. 24, No. 9 (November 1994), p. 11.

37. "Qian Qichen Concludes Visit to Israel on 18 September," *FBIS-China,* 22 September 1992, p. 14; Thomas L. Friedman, "China Warns U.S. on Taiwan Jet Deal," *New York Times,* 4 September 1992, p. A–3; Carol Giacomo, "U.S. Urges China to Reconsider Boycott of Arms Talks," Reuters, Ltd., 16 September 1992, p. 2; "Qian Qichen Arrives in Israel; Met by Peres," *FBIS-China,* 16 September 1992, pp. 11, 13; Barbara Crossette, "Many Empty Seats at Mideast Talks," *New York Times,* 12 May 1992, p. A–6; Harris, op. cit., pp. 260, 275; Harding, op. cit., p. 356.

38. William J. Clinton, "Report to Congress Concerning Extension of Waiver Authority for the People's Republic of China," 28 May 1993, *Public Papers of the Presidents of the United States* (Washinton: U.S. Government Printing Office, 1993), p. 774.

39. R. Jeffrey Smith and David B. Ottaway, "Spy Photos Suggest China Missile Trade," *Washington Post,* 3 July 1995, pp. A–1, A–17.

40. "Iraq Says China Vows to Work Against Sanctions," *The Washington Times,* 3 July 1995, p. A–8.

41. "China Tests Nuclear Bomb," *New York Times,* 16 May 1995, p. A–8.

42. Harris, op. cit., p. 260.

43. Barbara Crosette, "China Breaks Ranks with Other Nuclear Nations on Treaty," *New York Times,* 19 April 1995, p. A–16.

44. Harding, op. cit., p. 332.

45. Harris, op. cit., p. 168.

46. Harris, op. cit., p. 29; *The Economist,* 3 December 1994, p. 46.
47. Harris, op. cit., pp. 60, 83.
48. Harris, op. cit., pp. 47, 48.
49. Ibid., pp. 33, 66.
50. Ibid., p. 60.
51. John Calabrese, *China's Changing Relations with the Middle East,* op. cit., p. 45.
52. Harris, op. cit., p. 133.
53. Ibid., pp. 133, 214, 219, 232.
54. Schichor, op. cit., pp. 81, 82.
55. Schichor, op. cit., pp. 80, 81; Harris, op. cit., p. 109.
56. Schichor, op. cit., p. 81.
57. Schichor, op. cit., p. 81; Harris, op. cit., pp. 198, 199.
58. Schichor, op. cit., p. 82; Harris, op. cit., p. 199.
59. Schichor, op. cit., p. 88; "Riyadh and Beijing Declare Start of Full Diplomatic Ties," *New York Times,* 22 July 1990, p. I-6.
60. Harris, op. cit., p. 250; and "Resolution 678 of 29 November 1990," in *Resolutions and Decisions of the Security Council: 1990,* S/INF/46 (New York: United Nations, 1991), pp. 27, 28.
61. Harris, op. cit., pp. 212, 213.
62. John Calabrese, *China's Changing Relations with the Middle East* (London and New York: Pinter Publishers, 1991), p. 131.
63. Chinese purchases of Egyptian cotton also followed Premier Chou En-lai's 1963 visit. John Calabrese, *China's Changing Relations with the Middle East,* pp. 11, 12, 22, 23, 31; Harris, op. cit., p. 178.
64. Lally Weymouth, "The Peace Wheel Should Move: Egypt's Mubarak Nudges Israel and the PLO toward Compromise," *Washington Post,* 11 June 1995, p. C-2.
65. "Qian Returns from Trip," *FBIS-China,* 25 January 1994, p. 9.
66. "Statement by H. E. Qian Qichen, Vice-Premier and Minister of Foreign Affairs, and Chairman of the Delegation of the People's Republic of China at the Forty-ninth Session of the United Nations General Assembly, 28 September 1994," p. 2.
67. *The Economist,* 12 November 1994, p. 42; Wu Yu-Shan, "Taiwan in 1993: Attempting a Diplomatic Breakthrough," *Asian Survey,* Vol. 34, No. 1 (January 1994), pp. 53, 54.
68. Lillian Craig Harris, op. cit., p. 273; Nicholas D. Kristof, "The World: More Than One Way to Squeeze China," *New York Times,* 22 May 1994, p. IV-5.

69. Harry Harding, op. cit., pp. 159, 160.
70. Thomas L. Friedman, "Arab-Israel Talks on Regional Issues Start in Moscow." *New York Times,* 29 January 1992, p. A–1; Clyde Haberman, "Mideast Parley Ends in Moscow under Shadow: Palestinians Role Hazy as New Talks Are Set," *New York Times,* 30 January 1992, p. A–1; Thomas L. Friedman, "Mideast Session Adjourns, with Prospects Uncertain for Second Phase of Talks," *New York Times,* 2 November 1991, p. 1; and Friedman, "Israel and Arabs, Face to Face, Begin Quest for Mideast Peace: First Full Meeting," *New York Times,* 31 October 1991, p. A–1.
71. Lillian Craig Harris, op. cit., pp. 264, 265.
72. Warren Christopher, "U.S. National Interest in the Asia-Pacific Region," Address by the Secretary of State to the National Press Club, Washington, D.C., 28 July 1995, pp. 4, 5.
73. Martin Sieff, "Anger at U.S. Brings China, Russia Closer: Resentment Centers on Human Rights," *Washington Times,* 3 July 1995, pp. A–1, A–8.
74. Senator Bill Bradley, "Floor Statement by Senator Bill Bradley on China's Most Favored Nation Status," 18 May 1994, p. 5.
75. Harris, op. cit., p. 180; Harding, op. cit., pp. 93, 270, 334.
76. David Zweig, "Clinton and China: Creating a Policy Agenda that Works," *Current History,* Vol. 92, No. 575 (September 1993), p. 249.
77. Hemen Ray, *China and Eastern Europe* (New Delhi: Radiant Publishers, 1988), pp. 3, 5, 121, 122.
78. Craig R. Whitney, "U.S. and 4 Other Big Arms Makers Adopt Guidelines on Sales," *New York Times,* 20 October 1991, p. 11.
79. "Full Text of PRC-French Communiqué," *FBIS-China,* 12 January 1994, p. 10.
80. Sir Leon Brittan, "European Commission Launches New Policy on China," 5 July 1995, Reference IP/95/731, p. 1; and "EU Calls for U.S., China to Soften Dispute on WTO," *The Wall Street Journal,* 6 July 1995, p. A–5.
81. "Text of Jiang Zemin's 'Reunification' Speech," *FBIS-China,* 30 January 1995, p. 85.
82. "Text of President Lee Teng-hui's Unification Speech," *FBIS-China,* 10 April 1995, p. 79.
83. Lee Teng-hui, "Always in My Heart: An Olin Lecture," delivered at Cornell University, Ithaca, New York, 9 June 1995, p. 8; and Daniel Southerland, "Lee Visit Turns into a Balancing Act," *Washington Post,* 10 June 1995, p. A–8.

84. "Jiang Urges Relations with U.S. Based on Equality," *FBIS-China,* 18 January 1995, p. 4.
85. Zweig, op. cit., p. 250; Gerald Segal, editor, *China in the Nineties: Crisis Management and Beyond* (Oxford: Clarendon Press), p. 180.
86. Harding, op. cit., p. 359.
87. Harding, op. cit., . 94; Schichor, op. Cit., p. 89.
88. Harris, op. cit., p. 271.
89. Joan E. Spero, under secretary for economic and agricultural affairs, "The International Economic Agenda and the State Department's Role: Excerpts from Address before the Congressional International Economic Issues Forum, Washington, D.C., February 25, 1994," *U.S. Department of State Dispatch,* 7 March 1994, Vol. 5, No. 10, p. 123.
90. Christopher, op. cit., p. 7.
91. The four agreements which established: (1) a system of regular meetings; (2) the cross-delivery of registered letters; (3) the verification of official documents issued by the other side; and (4) an agenda of topics to be addressed in the future. Nicholas D. Kristof, "Starting to Build Their First Bridge, China and Taiwan Sign 4 Pacts," *New York Times,* 30 April 1993, p. A–11.
92. Martin Sieff, "China Recalls Envoy to U.S.; Aims to Head Off Opening to Taiwan," *The Washington Times,* 17 June 1995, p. A–14.
93. Seth Faison, "Taiwan Reports Nearby Firing of 4 Test Missiles by China," *New York Times,* 24 July 1995, p. A–2; and "China Asks Clinton to Reaffirm Policy on Taiwan's Status," *New York Times,* 13 July 1995, p. 1.
94. Warren Christopher, "U.S. National Interest in the Asia-Pacific Region," Address by the Secretary of State to the National Press Club, Washington, D.C., 28 July 1995, p. 13.
95. Harris, op. cit., p. 264.

II / Sino-American Trade and Diplomacy

It is possible that the Clinton Administration would seize an opportunity for a presidential visit to China before its reelection campaign intensifies. But as correspondent Patrick E. Tyler explained in *The New York Times* on December 19, 1994, China's human-rights policies have heretofore precluded a presidential visit.[1]

The question of human rights in China—i.e., the lack of progress thereupon—represents the biggest obstacle to an improvement of Sino-American relations. When Secretary of State Christopher met with PRC Foreign Minister Qian Qichen—at the United Nations, on 17 April 1995—human rights questions are reported to have predominated in Mr. Christopher's requests.[2]

Because the United States is the leading Western power in championing the cause of China's human rights, a current and comprehensive history of Sino-American diplomacy might provide the best framework for a review of the existing human-rights situation.

An Overview of Sino-American Diplomacy

The most important human-rights policy pronouncement to come from the Clinton Administration was put forth on 28 May 1993, in the form of Presidential Executive

Order 12850. President Clinton outlined his decision to link the Most-Favored-Nation and human rights questions thusly:

> The core of this policy will be a resolute insistence upon significant progress on human rights in China. To implement this policy, I am signing today an Executive Order that will have the effect of extending most-favored-nation status for China for 12 months. Whether I extend MFN next year, however, will depend upon whether China makes significant progress in improving its human rights record.[3]

This document—formally titled "Conditions for Renewal of Most-Favored-Nation Status for the People's Republic of China in 1994"—comprised four sections. Section One is the one to which news reporters and China experts most frequently referred. It stipulated that "the Secretary of State shall make a recommendation to the President to extend or not to extend MFN status to China for the 12-month period beginning July 3, 1994."[4]

The executive order also outlined seven human-rights areas, upon which the Chinese People's Republic would have to act in order to renew once again its MFN trading status in May of 1994. Two of the seven topics were deemed as "mandatory"; the remaining five were deemed as important but somewhat less obligatory, requiring a demonstration of "overall, significant progress" in order to satisfy policymakers in Washington.[5]

Paragraph A of Section One outlined the two mandatory conditions for MFN renewal: (1) "freedom of emigration" under section 402 (i.e., the Jackson-Vanik Amendment) of the 1974 Trade Act; and (2) Chinese compliance with "the 1992 bilateral agreement between the United States and China concerning prison labor."[6]

Paragraph B of Section One outlined five steps upon which the United States sought "overall, significant progress." The five steps required: (1) adherence to the Universal Declaration of Human Rights; (2) "releasing and providing an acceptable accounting for Chinese citizens imprisoned or detained for the nonviolent expression of their political and religious beliefs, including such expression of beliefs in connection with the Democracy Wall and Tiananmen Square movements"; (3) the "humane treatment of prisoners, such as by allowing access to prisons by international humanitarian and human rights organizations"; (4) the protection of "Tibet's distinctive religious and cultural heritage"; and (5) the permission of "international radio and television broadcasts into China."[7]

The confidence with which America advanced these precepts was based on commercial trends: the steadily increasing dependence of China on bilateral trade with the United States, especially in the area of light manufactured goods. Since President Carter's decision in the middle of 1980 to establish an MFN (Most-Favored-Nation) arrangement between Beijing and Washington, bilateral trade had skyrocketed from $1.1 billion in 1978 to $2.3 billion in 1979, to $4.9 billion in 1980, to $5.5 billion in 1981. After a reduction in the early 1980s—to $4.4 billion in 1983—bilateral trade rose to $13.5 billion in 1988. By 1992, China had accrued an $18.2 billion trade surplus with the United States.[8]

At the time of President Clinton's executive order, statistics indicated that China needed the United States' market more than the United States needed China. The United States had become China's third largest trading partner, after Hong Kong and Japan. Conversely, China ranked as America's fourteenth largest trading partner, and occupied only 1.7 percent of America's bilateral trade as of 1988.[9]

Dr. Harry Harding explained that "without MFN status, Chinese exports to the United States were subject to the high tariffs provided by the Smoot-Hawley Act of 1930."[10] And Joan Spero—the U.S. Under Secretary of State for Economic and Agricultural Affairs—clarified the Clinton Administration's attitude on 25 February 1994, in an address before the Congressional International Economic Issues Forum in Washington, D.C.

> As we work to accomplish other foreign policy objectives, from human rights to non-proliferation to protection of the environment, our economic ties increasingly will be seen . . . as providing the leverage we need to produce change in non-economic areas.[11]

These terms of bilateral trade, however, did not induce immediate Chinese cooperation on human-rights questions. This was explained by Dennis A. Rondinelli, in his work titled *Expanding Sino-American Business and Trade:*

> China took particular offense at linking human-rights practices with trade restrictions and especially with continuation of MFN status. The PRC's position was that the United States' insistence that its trading partners meet its human-rights standards was selective. It used human-rights standards as a condition for approving MFN status in China but not in other countries that had worse records. Chinese officials argued that in many aspects of human rights, such as crime rates and racial discrimination, China has a better record than the United States. One Chinese legal expert argued that the United States "adopts one criterion to judge itself and another to judge the rest of the world."[12]

In a collaborative analysis dated 29 May 1994, *The New York Times* reported that after the promulgation of Executive Order 12850, Sino-American relations did not improve or even maintain the *status quo ante,* but continued to deteriorate. Specifically, the Chinese: (1) loaded chemicals for making weapons on a freighter heading for Iran; (2) shipped M-11 missile technology to Pakistan, in violation of an international missile agreement; and (3) rejected the Clinton administration's requests to cancel a long-scheduled underground nuclear test.[13]

Current U.S. Diplomacy toward China, from 1994 to the Present

In an attempt to reverse the downward spiral of Sino-American relations, the Clinton Administration launched a series of Congressional and cabinet-level initiatives in 1994. The first five-month period of this diplomacy was designed to improve relations in order to facilitate a favorable MFN assessment by the president in late May of 1994. The remainder of 1994 was devoted to the renewal of substantive bilateral contacts.

The rationale underpinning this policy was subsequently outlined by Montana Senator Max Baucus, in an address to the Business Coalition for U.S.–China Trade in Washington, D.C. His speech—titled "China Policy in the Age of Pacific Community"—was delivered on 19 January 1995. In reference to the current Chinese leadership question, Senator Baucus seemed to differentiate the first and second segments of 1994:

. . . until the transition is over, we will see something close to paralysis. It is a frustrating time. It may continue for years, and we must be patient. But we cannot afford to be passive. In these years, we must lay a foundation. We must explain to the present government, and all those who hope to succeed it, what we expect *from* China and we must show the Chinese public what we hope to see *for* China.[14]

In January 1994, there were a number of cabinet- and subcabinet-level contacts between Beijing and Washington. They included: (1) Treasury Secretary Lloyd Bentsen's visit to Beijing, to discuss trade issues; (2) Under Secretary of State Lynn Davis's meeting in Washington, D.C., with Deputy Foreign Minister Liu Huaqiu, to discuss China's ballistic missile exports; and (3) Secretary of State Warren Christopher's European meeting with PRC Foreign Minister Qian Qichen.[15]

In addition to these cabinet-level contacts, a U.S. Congressional delegation also visited China in January of 1994. On 15 January 1994, President Jiang Zemin told a Congressional delegation that the PRC would strive to satisfy President Clinton's human rights requests in the following months. President Jiang also added that Beijing opposed the linkage of human rights with the Sino-American trade relationship. The delegation also met with Economic Minister Zhu Rongji. The all-Democratic delegation—which visited Beijing at President Clinton's request—was led by House Majority Leader Richard A. Gephardt, and comprised five other members of the House of Representatives.[16]

Secretary Bentsen's January 1994 Visit to Beijing

The most important contact of the new year, however, occurred in Beijing from 20 to 24 January. In what was then the highest-level visit to China ever conducted by a Clinton Administration official, Treasury Secretary Lloyd Bentsen met in Beijing with Prime Minister Li Peng, Central Bank Governor Zhu Rongji, and Finance Minister Liu Xhongli.[17]

Secretary Bentsen's primary aim was the completion of a new agreement restricting the use of Chinese prison labor to make export products. This PRC practice—which continues today—contravenes such United States trade legislation as Section 307 of the 1930 Smoot-Hawley Tariff Act. The prison labor issue was central to president Clinton's human-rights agenda; it impelled both U.S. Treasury and PRC officials to negotiate for two months toward the elaboration of a Chinese-American Prison Labor Memorandum of Understanding, dated 7 August 1992. The United States sought to increase to thirty the number of visits allowed to Chinese prisons suspected of exploiting prison labor.[18]

The factories notorious for the use of prison labor were suspected to have included: (1) the Shanghai Lao-Dong Steel Pipe Works; (2) the Beijing Qing-He Hosiery Factory; (3) the Xiang-Yang Machinery Plant, in the Hubei Province; and (4) the Golden Horse Diesel Factory, in the Yunnan Province. The Shanghai Lao-Dong Steel Pipe Works produced welded steel pipe, galvanizing steel pipe and adjustable wrenches. The Beijing Qing-He Hosiery Factory produced child and adult apparel. The Xiang-Yang Machinery Plant produced planing, shaping, and slotting machines. The Golden Horse Diesel Factory manufactured diesel engines. (The entry of these products into the United States of America had been withheld by the U.S. Customs Service in 1991 and 1992 because of their production in Chinese prisons.)[19]

On the first day of his visit—20 January—Secretary Bentsen delivered a speech to two hundred academics at the Chinese Academy of Social Sciences. He used this occasion to proclaim that the PRC authorities had agreed to reopen their prisons to American customs officers to ensure that the prison factories were not making products for export to the United States. Specifically, the PRC agreed to permit inspections of five prisons alleged to be producing goods for export. (The 1992 agreement, consummated by the Bush Administration, fell into disuse after only two inspections. Domestically, the U.S. Customs Service had been invoking the provisions of 18 U.S. Code 1761 to penalize American companies that wittingly imported unmarked prison goods from China.)[20]

On Friday, January 21st, Secretary Bentsen met with Zhu Rongji to preside over the eighth session of a rejuvenated China–United States Joint Economic Commission. This bilateral body had been used to resolve economic differences—e.g., the resolution of currency-control differences—but was suspended after the Tiananmen Square massacre of 4 June 1989.[21]

The Joint Economic Commission, established by Jimmy Carter and Deng Xiao-ping during the latter's visit to the United States in January 1979, had met seven times from 1980 to 1987. Leading the Chinese side was PRC Finance Minister Liu Zhongli; leading the U.S. delegation was Secretary Bentsen. Messrs. Bentsen and Liu co-chaired a meeting that produced a thirteen-point statement outlining future cooperation.[22]

Of secondary importance was an agreement by the PRC to stop the circumvention of U.S. quotas on Chinese textile exports by shipping them through third countries. The textile transshipment question applied not just to Hong Kong, but to U.S. import quotas assigned to such Middle Eastern nations as Lebanon and Kuwait. This circumvention would be stemmed in part by U.S. customs inspection on Chinese soil. The new textile agreement applied for the first time to silk garments as well.[23]

Of tertiary significance were other human-rights concerns: (1) the release of political prisoners from Tibet's and China's democracy movements; and (2) the initiation of a dialogue between the PRC and the International Red Cross on visits to prisoners.[24]

That Secretary Bentsen's trip was economically productive was as clear then as it is now. Its connection to progress on human-rights issues, however, was only underscored two months later. On 18 March 1994—en route to a Honolulu, Hawaii meeting of seventeen Pacific Rim finance ministers—the Treasury Secretary proclaimed that were President Clinton to decide at that time whether to renew China's MFN status, that he would not do so because of Beijing's human rights behavior. Mr. Bentsen's comments were made in Los Angeles.[25]

Although Secretary Bentsen's exploits dominated the Sino-American dialogue in January of 1994, the burden of the preparations that preceded President Clinton's momentous MFN decision in May were conducted by the United States Department of State. The first U.S. diplomatic pronouncement of 1994 appeared in an interview published in *The New York Times* on 1 January. J. Stapleton Roy—the American ambassador to China—claimed to correspondent Patrick E. Tyler that the "vast bulk" of political prisoners seized in the 1989 Tiananmen Square crackdown had been released.[26]

The State Department's disposition toward the Chinese human-rights question, however, was not so sanguine. On 3 January 1994, Winston Lord—the Assistant Secretary of State for East Asian and Pacific Affairs—warned that China's trade privileges would be revoked if Beijing could not convince Washington of "overall, significant progress" in its human-rights situation before June of 1994. Mr. Lord reaffirmed the importance of this progress on 24 February 1994, during an appearance before the Subcommittee on Trade of the House Ways and Means Committee. And on 11 January 1994, *New York Times* correspondent Elaine Sciolino reported that a draft of the State Department report on human rights concluded that China hadn't made sufficient progress to warrant a renewal of its Most-Favored-Nation trading status.[27]

Ambassador Roy's comments were made in late December 1993, more than three months after leading dissident Wei Jingsheng had been released from prison. It was an unauthorized meeting with Mr. Wei—on 27 February 1994—that provided the most controversial initiative of the year. John Shattuck—the Assistant Secretary of State for Democracy, Human Rights and Labor—met for forty-five minutes with Mr. Wei, in the first official U.S. encounter with the famous democracy advocate since his release from 14 ½ years in prison.[28]

On 24 and 25 January, Secretary of State Warren Christopher met with PRC Foreign Minister Qian Qichen in Paris. During his Paris rendezvous with Secretary Christopher, Foreign Minister Qian promised that China would set a precedent by providing detailed information on the list of 235 Chinese political prisoners compiled by Washington in the fall of 1993. As it remains today, a large-scale release of these prisoners was the ultimate objective of this information exchange.[29]

The Paris meeting, however, did yield an incremental improvement in China's human-rights posture. On 4 February 1994, *The New York Times* reported that China had released three political prisoners connected with the 1989 Tiananmen Square democracy movement. The three prisoners were: (1) Xiao Bin, a foreign television interviewer;

(2) Ding Junze, a philosophy instructor at a university in the Shanxi Province; and (3) Liao Yiwu, a leading poet in Sichuan Province who had produced a prodemocracy art video.[30]

Less than two months later—from 11 to 14 March 1994—the two diplomats would meet again, this time in Beijing. During Secretary of State Christopher's visit, he was accompanied by Ambassador Stapleton Roy, Undersecretary of State Lynn Davis; and Undersecretary of Defense Frank Wisner. PRC Foreign Minister Qian Qichen was accompanied by Vice Foreign Minister Tian Zengpei and Xu Huizi, the Deputy Chief of Staff of the Chinese People's Liberation Army.[31]

The Secretary of State's second encounter with the PRC Foreign Minister—which was much maligned by the American academic and business communities—finalized two important agreements, and facilitated the President's positive assessment toward the renewal of China's Most-Favored-Nation trading status.

Secretary Christopher's March 1994 Visit to Beijing

On 14 March 1994—after three days of bilateral discussions in Beijing—the U.S. delegation received substantive data on 235 specific cases of political prisoners. This data had been requested by the United States twice: once in the fall of 1993, and during the Paris meeting of 24 and 25 January 1994.

Moreover, the two sides codified an agreement to reopen prisons to American inspectors to insure against production for export to the United States. This agreement—titled a "Statement of Cooperation on the Implementation of the Memorandum of Understanding Between the

United States of America and the People's Republic of China on Prohibiting Import and Export Trade in Prison Labor Products"—had been reached in principle with Treasury Secretary Lloyd Bentsen in Beijing in January. This "Joint Statement" committed the Chinese to comply with the Memorandum of Understanding of 7 August 1992. It authorized American visits to all facilities, including labor camps, within sixty days of China's receipt of a written request from the United States. Finally, the "Joint Statement" compelled China to respond with a written report of investigation, within sixty days of receiving an American presentation of evidence of prison labor.[32]

Secretary Christopher's procurement of these two concessions by China—on the prisoners and prison labor—essentially enabled President Clinton to maintain the MFN status that is crucial to Sino-American trade.

Bilateral differences emerged in Beijing, however, when America attempted to compel China toward sweeping changes in its human-rights policies. In retrospect, it is clear that the events immediately preceding the Beijing bilaterals had effectively precluded this endeavour.

On 4 March 1994, President Clinton condemned the detention of Wei Jingsheng and several other dissidents. Joseph Fewsmith wrote in *Current History* that "by the time Christopher arrived in Beijing on March 11, at least 15 dissidents had been detained and others (including Tiananmen demonstration leader Wang Dan) had been encouraged to leave Beijing." Another dissident—Prof. Xu Liangying—had wanted to arrange a meeting with the U.S. Secretary of State. The seventy-four-year-old academician complained, however, that he was placed under house arrest and was restricted to his apartment in Beijing's university district.[33]

Clinton Administration officials also said that the detentions could alter Secretary of State Christopher's plans to visit China in the following week. Although the visit was a productive one, the human-rights confrontation clouded the atmosphere. On 12 March 1994, Chinese officials rejected the United States's concept of human rights and warned against linking China's Most-Favored-Nation status to its human-rights policies.[34]

Sino-American viewpoints on the human-rights question diverged diametrically. Plans for a joint news conference were cancelled after ninety minutes of talks at the Diaoyutai State Guesthouse. Instead, Foreign Minister Qian Qichen and Secretary of State Christopher conducted concurrent but separate briefings. Foreign Minister Qian explained at that time that "Sino-American relations are not only bilateral relations but should be put in the global context and that the future and the 21st century should be kept in mind in handling the relations."[35]

So as to underscore the intractability of this impasse—on 20 March 1994—Foreign Minister Qian Qichen said that the importance of China's trade with the United States had been exaggerated, and added that China was ready to return to the Cold War status of no trade relations with the United States if the human-rights-related disagreements could not be resolved.[36]

Foreign Minister Qian was referring to the American embargo, which was maintained from 1950 until 27 February 1972, when visiting U.S. President Richard Nixon joined PRC Premier Chou En-lai in signing the Shanghai communiqué to reopen bilateral commercial transactions. In *Expanding Sino-American Business and Trade,* Dennis A. Rondinelli explained that "from 1949 until the initiation of the 'open-door' policy in 1978, only the government's fourteen centrally controlled foreign trade corporations (FTCs) could export products; and stringent restrictions were placed on imports and foreign investment."[37] A return to this arrangement would have created a tremendous disruption in each country's commerce.

Pronouncements such as Foreign Minister Qian's made it clear that China had perceived Secretary Christopher's human-rights demands as a form of arrogant American interference and intrusion in its internal affairs. There was, however, a political dimension that weighed as heavily in China's decision-making.

In a "News Analysis" which appeared in the 14 March 1994 issue of *The New York Times,* correspondent Patrick E. Tyler explained that the Secretary of State's visit coincided with the annually convened National People's Congress. It was thus possible that this coincidence compelled China's leaders to maintain an inflexible demeanour toward the American initiatives, lest they "lose face" in front of the assembled Chinese legislators.[38]

Patrick E. Tyler also explained that the U.S. officials were keenly alert to this possibility, but that scheduling pressures subordinated such sensitivities to the demands of the globally driven agenda that confronts every Secretary of State.[39]

So as to build on the fundamental success of his thankless diplomatic foray, Secretary of State Christopher persevered by proxy. On 19 May 1994, it was reported that Michael H. Armacost—a former ambassador to Japan and Under Secretary of State—had been sent as a secret envoy to Beijing to advocate the areas of human rights remaining on Presidential Executive Order 12850.[40]

Ambassador Armacost's secret diplomacy reaped dividends. On 6 April, Foreign Minister Qian responded to Secretary Christopher's earlier request by publicly affirming China's adherence to the Universal Declaration of Human Rights.[41]

Thus was the stage set for President Clinton's MFN decision in May. The congressional and commercial pressures that converged on the Clinton Administration's policymakers will be addressed in the section that follows.

President Clinton's May 1994 MFN Decision

On 26 May 1994, President Clinton proclaimed his decision toward trade with China. He began by stating that "over $8 billion of United States exports to China last year supported over 150,000 America jobs." Upon this premise, he abandoned the linkage between bilateral trade and progress on human rights. His renewal of China's Most-Favored-Nation trading status was unconditional:

> I am moving, therefore, to delink human rights from the annual extension of Most-Favored-Nation trading status for China. That linkage has been constructive during the past year. But I believe, based on our aggressive contacts with the Chinese in the past several months, that we have reached the end of the usefulness of that policy and it is time to take a new path toward the achievement of our constant objectives. We need to place our relationship into a larger and more productive framework.[42]

President Clinton did, however, maintain President Bush's ban on the shipment of U.S. weapons to the Chinese military. He also prohibited the importation of Chinese guns and ammunition to the United States. This was because (as of May 1994) the importation of guns and ammunition from the PRC was producing $200 million in revenue per annum.[43]

Wu Jianmin, the PRC Foreign Ministry spokesman, met

68

twice with foreign journalists on 27 May 1994 to welcome the renewal of China's MFN status. While Mr. Wu was careful not to characterize the American decision as a victory for China, he did urge an end to the nontrade sanctions that were imposed immediately after the 1989 Tiananmen crackdown.[44]

The Clinton Administration's decision was engendered by competing pressures from the Executive Branch, the Legislative Branch, and the business community. On 29 January 1994, Robert E. Rubin—the director of the National Economic Council—urged President Clinton to delink its trade and human-rights requests to China.

The president took a step toward delinkage on 24 March 1994, during a news conference. After restating the importance of observing strict standards for the improvement of China's human-rights behavior, President Clinton hinted that it would be possible to renew China's MFN status if the PRC could meet the minimum human rights standards outlined in his Executive Order of May 1993.[45]

Less than a week later—on 30 March 1994—there was yet another hint of greater American flexibility. After a speech to the United States Chamber of Commerce, Assistant Secretary of State Winston Lord said that the Clinton Administration could consider a selective withdrawal of current trade privileges from the PRC's state-owned enterprises, vis-à-vis an across-the-board penalty if the PRC's progress (on human rights) were to be deemed insufficient. *New York Times* correspondent Steven Greenhouse reported that this suggestion drew immediate support from, *inter alios,* Mr. Richard Brecher, the director of business advisory services at the United States–China Business Council.[46]

On 2 May 1994, President Clinton met with Zou Jiahua—the PRC Deputy Prime Minister—to implore China to do more to improve its human rights record before the 3 June deadline. Although no new commitment was offered by Mr. Zou during the forty-minute meeting in the Oval Office, the PRC made two timely concessions within the following fortnight.

The first concession comprised a series of political-prisoner releases. On 10 May 1994, *The New York Times* reported that Yu Haocheng—a onetime constitutional expert and Communist propaganda chief—would be allowed to leave China in May to study and lecture at Columbia University. This followed the eleventh petition made by Mr. Yu to the Communist authorities. Mr. Yu, then sixty-six, was the chief editor of the Masses Publishing House, an organ of China's Public Security Bureau. His requests were broached in 1992, after three years of imprisonment and detention under house arrest.[47]

On 12 May 1994, a fifty-four-year-old woman, imprisoned for four years for religious activities, was released in southern China's Fujian Province. This was followed by the release—on 13 May 1994—of five religious activists from labor camps for "good behaviour." Then on 14 May 1994, the PRC released Chen Ziming, a forty-two-year-old social scientist and publisher, on medical parole. Mr. Chen—along with Wang Jungtao—had received a thirteen-year prison term in February 1991. China's decision was seen as an effort to comply with part of President Clinton's May 1993 executive order on human rights in China.[48]

The second concession came on 17 May 1994, when the PRC agreed to allow a visit by a team of American technicians to discuss the cessation of jamming of Voice of America radio broadcasts. This concession was also one of seven human rights demands set by President Clinton in 1993, and one of five demands upon which the Clinton administration had requested "significant progress."[49]

It is also likely that Deputy Prime Minister Zou used his visit to the White House to draw an economic parallel between the concurrent situation and that of May 1989, when the 26 percent annual inflation rate, rapid consumer prices, and evidence of corruption brought Beijing to a standstill before the Tiananmen Square massacre of 4 June. In early 1994, the Chinese government had: (1) reimposed price controls on twenty basic commodities, to combat inflation; and (2) banned all new construction on major projects and luxury projects (e.g., golf courses and race-tracks).[50]

Another Oval Office meeting—this time between the President and his Secretary of State—transpired exactly three weeks later on 23 May. The Clinton-Christopher dialogue was conducted in accordance with Section Two of the May 1993 Executive Order, which stated that the Secretary of State was to "submit his recommendation to the President before June 3, 1994." Secretary Christopher's May 23rd report deemed as satisfactory the PRC's treatment of the two mandatory conditions on the May 1993 Executive Order. The report qualified, however, that there had been insufficient overall progress on the remaining five areas outlined in that same Executive Order.[51]

The Clinton Administration's decision to renew China's MFN privileges was heavily influenced by both houses of Congress. This factor was identified by the President in his speech on 26 May:

> The MFN law basically is tied to emigration, and we have successfully resolved all outstanding emigration cases with the Chinese. Why was it extended to involve human rights here? **Because of the frustration in the Congress** that the previous administration had reestablished relationships too quickly after Tiananmen Square, and there seemed to

be no other aggressive human rights strategy.[52] (Emphasis added)

On 21 April 1994, *The New York Times* reported that Democratic leaders were cooperating with the White House to reach a compromise that would sustain China's MFN status while enacting limited sanctions should the PRC fail to satisfy all of the objectives on the Clinton Administration's human rights agenda for China. The proposal, which Winston Lord broached on 30 March—for selective sanctions in lieu of sweeping penalties—was endorsed by Representative Robert Matsui, a California Democrat supporting China's MFN renewal.[53]

Congressional consul, however, antedated Assistant Secretary Lord's overture. On 27 January 1994, Senator Max Baucus delivered a speech to the U.S.–China Business Council opposing the use of tariff's to influence China's human-rights behavior. At that time, the Montana Democrat chaired the Senate subcommittee on international trade. Montana is a major exporter of wheat to China. In his speech—titled "Where We Stand and Where We Go From Here: China Policy in 1994 and Beyond"—the Senator approximated U.S. exports to China at $9 billion per year. Cancellation of this bilateral trade would have affected roughly 180,000 American jobs. Senator Baucus perceived the MFN bargaining tactic as an antique of the Cold War:

MFN is an outdated tool. The core MFN law, the Jackson-Vanik Amendment, is a Cold War law dealing with the right of Soviet Jews to emigrate. It is an anachronism, and the time has come to put it behind us for good. President Clinton's Executive Order was right for last spring. The alternative was a permanent conditions law, not unconditional MFN. But a new Executive Order is not right for this spring. Perpetually threatening the economic equivalent of nuclear war is not sound policy.[54]

Senator Baucus's convictions were seconded on 10 May 1994, during a speech at the American Enterprise Institute by Rep. Lee H. Hamilton. Mr. Hamilton—who was the chairman of the House Foreign Affairs Committee—implored the Administration to stop using trade sanctions and search for other, more suitable means of promoting human rights. His speech—titled "The United States and China: Toward a Policy of Realism"—included the following observation:

> Whatever leverage MFN conditionality has provided in the past year, its application in this next phase would probably be counterproductive. It is time to de-link. We should also continue to promote human rights in China. The tools are there: we can foster change through personal diplomacy and our economic ties; we can work in multilateral forums; we can establish a bilateral human rights commission.[55]

Shortly thereafter—on 18 May 1994—House Speaker Thomas S. Foley said that the withdrawal of China's MFN benefits would cause a trade disruption. This attitude was restated on the same day by New Jersey Senator Bill Bradley. In a floor statement to the Senate, the New Jersey Democrat called the link between human rights and trade privileges "Cold War old-think." Senator Bradley implored President Clinton "to free China policy from the Cold War straight jacket embodied in the MFN-human rights linkage" and "to pursue a more multi-faceted approach to U.S.–China relations."[56]

On 25 May 1994 in *The New York Times* editorial entitled "Trade, the Real Engine of Democracy"—Senator

Bradley urged President Clinton to abandon the obsolescent mandatory linkage between human rights and bilateral trade. In its stead, the New Jersey Senator suggested a strategy of comprehensive and flexible engagement.[57]

Immediately after the Clinton Administration's decision, Samuel R. Berger—the Deputy National Security Adviser—appeared on "Good Morning America." Mr. Berger assured correspondent Charles Gibson that the Clinton Administration would continue "to press for a vigorous human rights policy in the context of policy of engagement with China."[58] The approaches favored by the Executive and Legislative Branches toward the pursuit of human-rights rectification, however, were not synchronized.

On 9 August 1994, the Clinton Administration was forced to thwart a campaign within the House of Representatives to restrict trade with China so as to punish the PRC for its human-rights violations. By a vote of 270 to 158, the House defeated a proposal to impose steep tariffs on imports from factories owned by the Chinese military.[59]

The congressional campaign had been driven largely by organized labor. On 13 April 1994, Lane Kirkland—the president of the AFL-CIO—had accused the Chinese army and police of running factories to increase the PRC's defense budget. Mr. Kirkland had opposed an extension of the MFN trading status, because the Chinese military-industrial connection was a major source for American companies purchasing products from assault rifles to toilet seats, stuffed animals, shoes and household goods. This military-industrial phenomenon—along with its prison labor—had contributed to an American bilateral trade deficit with China that had ballooned from $300,000 in 1983 to $22.7 billion in 1994. *New York Times* correspondent Edward A. Gargan wrote that this deficit was second only to America's $59.32 billion deficit with Japan. According to the AFL-CIO, an extension of MFN privileges would support these trends, and would thusly have continued to take jobs from American workers.[60]

President Kirkland's concerns centered upon conglomerates, such as Poly Technologies Incorporated, which is an affiliate of the China International Trust and Investment Corporation. Lillian Craig Harris wrote that it is "the arms sale and procurement agency for the People's Liberation Army and thus able to fill urgent orders direct from PLA stocks, an efficiency further enhanced by particularly close connections to the CCP leadership." Another arms company—the China North Industries Corporation (Norinoco)—is the trading arm of the Ministry of Machine-Building.[61]

Arms exports aside, China's large and low-salaried work force had produced impressively in four labor-intensive industries: (1) miscellaneous manufactured articles; (2) machinery and transport equipment; (3) manufactured materials; and (4) mineral fuels. In each of these areas, Chinese exports enjoyed an advantage in the United States market. Investors from Taiwan and Hong Kong finance foreign enterprises and joint ventures in the special economic zones (e.g., Shenzhen) along China's southern and eastern coasts.[62]

Opposition from organized labor, however, was overcome by opposition from America's corporate investors to a removal of China's MFN status. One corporate lobbying group—the Business Coalition of U.S.–China Trade—comprises more than eight hundred U.S. companies, trade associations, consumer groups, and farm organizations that support the expansion of Sino-American trade. Dennis A. Rondinelli wrote that "between 1979 and 1992, American companies invested more than $6.3 billion in about 2,800 business ventures in China."[63]

These groups feared a retaliation on tariffs imposed upon U.S. exports entering the PRC. U.S. exports to China—which totalled $8.76 billion in 1993—included airplanes, fertilizer, wheat and automobiles.[64] Specifically, China could upgrade the classification of its tariffs upon U.S. goods from the "minimum" to the "general" category. In *Current History*, David Zweig explained that such an upgrade would have affected the "American aircraft industry, producers of chemical fertilizer, exporters of wheat and other grains, and producers of industrial construction machinery." (Other U.S. exports include transport equipment, food, and live animals.)[65]

American anxieties on the removal of MFN status applied as well to China's exports to the United States. By withholding MFN status, the Clinton Administration would have subjected Chinese imports to the steeper duties that were stipulated in the Smoot-Hawley Tariff Act of 1930.[66] According to Peter T. Mangione, the President of the Footwear Distributors and Retailers of America, an end to China's MFN access would have meant higher shoe prices, because the PRC provides more than half of all shoes sold in the United States, as well as 60 percent of all shoes imported by the United States.[67] As explained in *Expanding Sino-American Business and Trade:*

> Organizations sympathetic to continued MFN status for China estimate that the failure to renew it would increase the rate of duty on the top 25 dutiable Chinese imports from an average 18.7 percent to more than 50 percent. This would make more than half of the goods exported from China uncompetitive in the American market.[68]

The impact would have been most acute for the 150,000 to 200,000 American workers whose employment depended upon trade with China. This ominous potentiality was clarified to Secretary of State Christopher on 13 March 1994, when he met with American business executives in Beijing.[69]

The U.S. business perspective was repeated two days later, at a panel discussion in Washington, D.C., sponsored by the Council on Foreign Relations. Mr. Lawrence W. Clarkson—the Boeing Company's corporate vice president for planning and international development—used that March 15th venue to oppose any change in China's trade status. At the time, the Boeing Company had garnered from China contracts totalling $3.9 billion to manufacture 64 new airplanes. In addition, the Boeing Company projected $2 billion to $3 billion in potential orders in the immediate future. This immediate projection was made within the context of a longer-term projection: that China would become the world's third-largest aviation market by the year 2010, with a need approximating eight hundred airplanes worth $40 billion.[70]

Concern over contracting related directly to America's competitors for foreign investment in China. Germany is China's largest European trading partner. At the time of President Clinton's decision, Sino-German trade was projected at $17 billion for 1994. This projection represented a huge increase from the $10 billion in bilateral trade conducted between Bonn and Beijing in 1993. Sino-German trade ultimately reached $18 billion in 1994. And unlike their competitors in the United States, European, Canadian, and Japanese investors were not impeded by concerns over human rights in China. Nor were they averse to the provision of mixed credits and soft loans, for they had already done so for more than a thousand projects.[71]

A revealing example was provided by Mr. Robert S. O'Neil, the chief executive of the engineering firm of De

Leuw, Cather & Company. De Leuw, Cather & Company had worked on Shanghai's subway system since 1987, and was negotiating for the subway project in Guangzhou in the winter of 1994. The efforts of this American engineering firm, however, were eclipsed by a concurrent visit from German Chancellor Helmut Kohl. Specifically, Germany's concessionary loans—which were offered without human-rights admonitions—provided the edge that cost Mr. O'Neil and his company a big contract.[72]

This trend was underscored in the summer of 1994, when PRC Premier Li Peng led a delegation of 150 on a sixteen-day tour of Europe. The climax of this tour—from 4 to 9 July 1994—occurred in Germany, with which China signed nearly $3.5 billion of contracts and letters of intent. *New York Times* correspondent Ferdinand Protzman reported that two of Germany's largest concerns—the heavy-machinery firm Asea Brown Boveri A.G. and the electronics group Siemens A.G.—signed joint-venture agreements approximating the respective sums of $630 million and $1 billion.[73]

To forestall a further erosion of America's share of the Chinese market, President Clinton turned to the Department of Commerce. In October of 1993, the Commerce Department—in close conjunction with the U.S. Trade Representative—had successfully implored the Chinese Government to sign a Memorandum of Understanding (MOU) on market access. It was not until Secretary Ronald H. Brown visited China, however, that this access began to realize its promise.[74]

Secretary Brown's August–September 1994 Visit

Ms. Joan Spero—the Under Secretary of State for Economic and Agricultural Affairs—had outlined the Clinton Administration's attitude to commercial diplomacy on 25 February 1994:

> The first speech the President gave on foreign policy last year gave a clear indication that economics would play a central role in his foreign policy. In his speech, the President laid out five goals for our policy. The Administration's second goal is to open global markets. The President has said "we must compete, not retreat," and has backed it up by coming out forcefully for open markets and fair competition and against protectionism.[75]

With this precept in mind, Commerce Secretary Ron Brown led a Presidential trade mission of twenty-four American executives to China from August 27 through September 2. The American delegation was received and hosted by Ms. Wu Yi, the Minister of Foreign Trade and Economic Cooperation (MOFTEC). The U.S. delegation also visited Shanghai and Guangzhou.[76]

With the human-rights question decoupled from those of trade,[77] Secretary Brown could aggressively pursue his business objectives. Fifteen different contracts were signed during the visit. At the end of his visit to Beijing, he announced the signing of agreements approximating $5 billion with PRC government industries.

New York Times correspondent Patrick E. Tyler wrote that of this $4.9 billion total, more than $2 billion was consigned to American firms participating as joint-venture partners or equipment sellers. Pitney Bowes, the information firm, announced a $20 million contract with the Ministry of Posts and Telecommunications to assist in modernizing and automating 55,000 post offices in China.

Concurrently, International Business Machines concluded a contract approximating $20 million.[78]

On 29 August 1994, Westinghouse signed a $140 million agreement to provide two steam turbines for a 700-megawatt electrical power plant in the Jiangsu Province. On 31 August, Michael Jordan—Westinghouse's chief executive—visited the Shanghai Sheraton Hua Ting Hotel to formalize the largest joint venture project of the PRC's power-generation manufacturing industry. The agreement was concluded by: (1) the Shanghai Electric Corporation; and (2) the Westinghouse Electric Corporation. The principal signatories of the agreement were Messrs. Jordan and Mi Qiping, the Chairman of the Shanghai Electric Corporation.[79]

Another joint venture was a high-tech cooperation agreement, signed on 29 August in Beijing between: (1) China's Great Wall Industry Corporation; and (2) Tandem Computers, Inc. of the United States. The former is China's premier aerospace industry enterprise. This agreement set a precedent, as it was Great Wall's first joint venture with a foreign computer company. To promote and sell Tandem products, Great Wall will establish the "Great Wall Nonstop Computer Technology Ltd." In turn, Tandem will provide sales and technological training.[80]

Commercial projections through the year 2000 enabled U.S. firms to use the visit to compete for thirty-four Chinese projects, the value of which exceeded $47 billion.[81]

Under the aegis of the Joint Commission on Commerce and Trade (JCCT), MOFTEC Minister Wu and Commerce Secretary Brown signed an accord that provided a framework for commercial cooperation in priority sectors of Sino-American trade. In addition to this JCCT Framework Arrangement, seven new agreements were signed by the two ministers, regarding: (1) medical technology; (2) electric power; (3) aviation and airport infrastructure; (4) chemical products; (5) information technology; (6) motor vehicles; and (7) environmental technology.

One of the fourteen government-to-government projects concerned the technology inherent in the Water Resources Forecast System (WARFS). This would be applied to two major rivers in China. Since 1993, WARFS—which includes computer work stations and software—had provided accurate three-month forecasts in Egypt's Nile River. WARFs was to be installed on the Huai River and then on the Chang Jiang River, which is the longest in China. Its technology was to positively influence floods and droughts, as well as irrigation operations, and other man-made ecosystems.[82]

To increase bilateral commerce among small- and medium-sized firms, the PRC and USA agreed to establish: (1) a U.S. Commercial Center in Shanghai; and (2) a U.S.-Chinese Commercial Strategy Center in Washington, D.C. These two centers would be staffed by representatives of the Chinese and American governments and business communities. Finally, the Commercial Law Program was also expanded.[83]

Its single-minded, monetary-oriented focus made the trade mission an unqualified success. This success, however, did not satisfy all of the PRC's trading objectives. On 11 September 1994, *The China Daily* quoted Zhou Shijian—the deputy director of MOFTEC's Institute of International Trade—as urging the United States to ease existing trade sanctions on the PRC. Mr. Zhou wanted Washington to: (1) indefinitely extend its Most-Favored-Nation trading status; (2) end its America's ban on soft loans to China; and (3) end limits on high-technology exports to China. Specifically, Zhou Shijian sought an expansion from 32 to 45 in the number of categories of high-technology items available for export to China.[84]

Secretary Perry's October 1994 Visit

The export of high-technology items had directly and adversely affected military relations between China and the United States. In August 1993, the United States imposed sanctions on China for its November 1992 transfer of M-11 missile-related equipment to Pakistan. *New York Times* correspondent Elaine Sciolino wrote that the American sanctions—which approximated $1 billion—affected the projected launchings of seven commercial satellites on Chinese rockets.

In early January 1994, the White House authorized the Chinese to launch two commercial satellites. One satellite was produced by the Hughes Aircraft Company, the other manufactured by Martin Marietta. The Hughes Aircraft launching—which was reconfigured so as to omit sensitive coding equipment—placed an Australian communications satellite in orbit.[85]

As early as March of 1994, the Clinton Administration was pursuing plans to upgrade the Sino-American military relationship. Frank Wisner—the Under Secretary of Defense for Policy—accompanied Secretary of State Christopher to Beijing from 11 to 14 March. He was received by General Liu Huaqing, the Vice-Chairman of China's Central Military Commission. During his meeting with General Liu—who also serves as Deputy Foreign Minister—Mr. Wisner specified the types of Sino-American military cooperation that might result from progress on human rights. Given progress on the human-rights questions, the United States was prepared to: (1) conduct regular meetings between

Secretary of Defense William Perry and China's Defense Minister; (2) form a joint commission on the conversion of military technology to civilian use; (3) organize and engage in joint peacekeeping exercises; and (4) cooperate with China on disaster-relief projects.[86]

Under Secretary Wisner, however, was forced to reduce his agenda when it became clear that China was not prepared to honor the human-rights requests on President Clinton's executive order. During his March 1994 visit to Beijing, his agenda was limited to human rights and the conversion of defense industries.[87]

When Defense Secretary William J. Perry arrived in Beijing on 15 October—at the invitation of PRC Defense Minister Chi Haotian—he was accompanied by Under Secretary Wisner. He was also accompanied by senior officials form the State and Commere Departments, as well as the National Security Council. The Defense Secretary's fifty-member delegation included: Senators Samuel Nunn and John Warner; Assistant Defense Secretaries Joseph Nye and Sandi Stuart; and Assistant Secretary of State Winston Lord.[88]

During his three-day visit to China—the first by a Secretary of Defense since the crackdown at Tiananmen Square on 4 June 1989—Mr. Perry: (1) met with senior Chinese leaders; (2) delivered a speech at the National Defense University; (3) visited Wuhan and Chongqing; and (4) inaugurated an American-Chinese commission to expedite China's conversion from military to civilian industries.[89]

In addition to meeting with Defense Minister Chi Haotian, Defense Secretary Perry met with: (1) Jiang Zemin, the President and Chairman of the Central Military Commission; (2) Premier Li Peng; (3) Liu Hua-qing; and (4)

Ding Henggao, the Minister of Commission of Science, Technology, Industry for National Defense.[90]

On 17 October, Minister Ding Henggao and Secretary Perry co-chaired the first meeting of the Sino-American joint defense conversion commission. The cochairmen signed a statement of principles to guide the efforts of the joint commission.

On 18 October 1994, Defense Secretary William J. Perry implored China's military leadership to be more open about the PRC defense budget and planning so as to allay anxieties abroad. Toward this end, Mr. Perry is said to have suggested that China issue a White Paper on National Defense to clarify its intentions and to dispel misunderstandings.[91]

New York Times correspondent Michael R. Gordon reported that as part of a reciprocal information exchange, the Chinese agreed to send a military delegation to the Pentagon to outline their five-year defense projections.[92] Moreover, China signed a binding agreement not to sell its M-9 and M-11 missiles to Arab countries. Thereafter, the Clinton Administration allowed American aerospace firms to enter the Chinese market. The upshot was approximately $2 billion worth of satellite orders that would otherwise have been conceded to Germany.[93]

With visits to China in 1994 by the U.S. Secretaries of Treasury, Commerce, and Defense, Sino-American relations appeared to have turned toward a positive direction. The year ended, however, with an ominous pronouncement by Ambassador Mickey Kantor, the U.S. Trade Representative.

Sino-American Confrontations over Copyrights, Patents and Intellectual Property

On 31 December 1994, U.S. Trade Representative Mickey Kantor announced the prospect of punitive trade tariffs against China. This action was to be taken through the invocation of the "Special 301" provision of the 1974 Trade Act. The "Special 301" provision covers intellectual property, and requires that after an investigation of up to six months, the U.S. Trade Representative must determine whether a nation's trade policies are unreasonable.[94]

Specifically, the Clinton Administration threatened to impose retaliatory tariffs against $2.8 billion of Chinese exports to the United States if the PRC did not prevent further pirating of American computer software, music, and movies.

China responded with a New Year's Eve threat of her own. The Ministry of Foreign Trade and Economic Cooperation (MOFTEC) demanded that Washington immediately withdraw its threat to impose sanctions against Beijing. Otherwise, the PRC threatened, it would suspend: (1) talks on joint ventures with American auto makers; (2) talks on tariffs on imports of cassette tapes, compact discs, cigarettes, etc.; and (3) the applications of American companies and their subsidiaries to set up holding companies in China.[95]

These punitive prospects took a step closer to reality less than one month later. On 28 January 1995—after nine days of negotiation—Sino-American trade talks collapsed. Ambassador Kantor threatened to impose steep tariffs on the PRC's products if an agreement was not reached. Specifically, the United States demanded that China: (1) immediately end the pirating of American computer software, movies, and music; and that (2) it desist from allowing

Chinese businesses to affix ersatz American labels on consumer products.[96]

The Chinese government had refused to close its notorious twenty-nine factories in southern China. These factories had achieved their notoriety by annually producing 70 million compact discs and other counterfeit products. Because these products are sold not just in China but in other Asian nations, it is estimated that this practice—which is tantamount to thievery—costs American businesses $1 billion a year.[97]

Were such an agreement not consummated by a 4 February 1995 deadline, 100 percent tariffs were to be imposed within days on some Chinese exports. The February 4th deadline was to be imposed under the legal auspices of a "Special 301" clause. The exports were said to include consumer electronics, toys, and clothing.[98]

On 4 February 1995—after negotiators from the Office of the U.S. Trade Representative had engaged in twenty-one fruitless sessions over the previous two years—President Clinton imposed 100 percent punitive tariffs on more than $1 billion in Chinese goods. After announcing this, the largest trade sanctions in American history, he warned of further action. China responded with tariffs against American-made goods. The penalties imposed by each nation were to commence on 26 February. There were two reasons for the designation of this three-week delay. First, the interim period could facilitate further negotiation to forestall this confrontation. And second, goods shipped before the commencement of retaliatory tariffs would not be affected.[99]

Within twenty-four hours of his announcement imposing trade sanctions, U.S. Trade Representative Mickey Kantor reportedly received a letter from PRC Trade Minister Wu Yi indicating a desire to resume talks in Beijing. Sino-

American trade talks resumed on 6 February 1995. A U.S. negotiating team—led by Deputy Trade Representative Charlene Barshefsky—travelled to China on the 13th of February.[100]

China's planned retaliation was to be directed against imports of U.S.-made cigarettes, alcohol, and films. Also subject to punitive action would be American-made telephone switchboards and the negotiations over large automobile-assembly joint ventures. The latter two targets would respectively have: (1) cost millions of dollars to AT&T Corporation; and (2) presented an insurmountable disadvantage to the Ford Motor Company. This potentiality, once implemented, would mean an increased German and Japanese market share in mini-vans. It would also represent a serious setback to the Clinton Administration, which endeavored to expand the presence of American auto manufacturers in China.[101]

In selecting goods to be affected by the tariffs, the United States Trade Representative tried to target those that were produced by China's state-owned enterprises. In the 7 February 1995 issue of *The Wall Street Journal,* correspondent Craig S. Smith explained that the USTR targeted products that were so narrowly defined that no single company was to be exposed to more than one or two items. Toys and electronics—China's No. 1 and No. 2 exports to the United States—were excluded from the list, because doubling the tariff on these items would have hurt large and small retailers residing in America and would have upset many U.S. consumers as well. Winter clothes—a key item to be affected by the proposed punitive tariffs—were not to be manufactured for several months. Conversely, China took care to omit airplanes—which accounted for approximately $2 billion of America's exports to China in 1994—from its punitive tariff list. McDonnell Douglas has what *New York Times* correspondent David E. Sanger described as a "giant aircraft factory" in Shanghai. [102]

On 26 February 1995, the United States and China signed an agreement to end violations of intellectual property by the PRC. The property in question comprised movies, compact discs, and computer software. The agreement was negotiated and signed by Ambassador Charlene Barshefsky and Trade Minister Wu Yi. Ambassador Barshefsky stated that all quotas would be lifted, effective immediately. Trade Minister Wu, mindful of China's aspirations toward gaining membership in the World Trade Organization, pledged not only to close counterfeit CD factories, but also to desist from using the pirated software in Chinese government offices. [103]

Under the Sino-American agreement, China endorsed three measures: (1) immediate steps to curtail intellectual property infringements; (2) an improvement of enforcement methods to prevent future abuses; and (3) an increased access by U.S. producers to Chinese markets.

1. To protect American copyrights, patents, and trademarks, the Chinese (a) raided and closed seven factories, destroying millions of pirated compact discs and laser discs; (b) promised to move against and destroy other infringing factories within three months; and (c) to adopt new measures to prevent pirated products from being exported.

2. To improve enforcement methods to prevent future abuses, the Chinese agreed to: (a) create a customs enforcement system, modeled on the United States Customs Service; (b) clarify its intellectual property regulations to its business and legal professionals; and (c) ensure that American right holders will have access to Chinese courts to claim their rights.

3. To increase American access to the Chinese markets, the PRC will: (a) place no quotas on the importation of American audiovisual products; (b) allow American record companies to offer their entire catalogues in China, subject to censorship; (c) allow American companies to enter joint-venture arrangements to produce their goods in China, starting in Shanghai and Guangzhou and expanding to eleven other cities within five years.[104]

The three-week period extending from 4 to 26 February witnessed flexibility and sincere effort on both sides of the bargaining table. In *The Wall Street Journal,* correspondents Helene Cooper and Robert S. Greenberger reported that the United States initially demanded the closure of all twenty-nine of the factories producing counterfeit American products.[105]

Although China did not completely satisfy this demand, it did conduct raids against seven of twenty-nine CD factories identified by the United States as major offenders. These raids were conducted in the week preceding the February 26th announcement of the Sino-American agreement. The seven factories closed were at the top of the list of offenders. Two examples are posited here.

On 16 February, *Washington Post* correspondent Steven Mufson reported that the Dragon Arts Sound Company—located in Guangdong's Zhuhai special economic zone near Macao—was stripped of its business license. This factory was prosecuted for wholesaling counterfeit CDs. And on 26 February 1995—just under the trade-talk deadline between the PRC and the U.S.—Chinese officials announced the closure of the Shenfei Laser and Optical System Company. This company is infamous for its copyright violations in the production of counterfeit audio and video discs.[106]

These factory closures concurred with a sweeping ten-day raid in twenty-three Chinese provinces. In a report dated 16 February 1995, *Wall Street Journal* correspondent Kathy Chen reported that PRC officials seized more than 357,000 pirated recordings during these forays.

On 11 March 1995—while in Beijing for the formal signing of the intellectual property agreement—U.S. Trade Representative Mickey Kantor stated that he was also determined to enforce a 1992 agreement intended to reduce Chinese barriers to American computers, heavy machinery, textiles, beer and agricultural products.[107]

Sino-America sales in agricultural products also occupied an important place in the first half of 1995. On 7 February, the Clinton Administration announced that it would expand subsidized wheat sales to Beijing, so as to preclude a bigger market share for European farm exports. Consequently, the PRC will pay approximately $20 million less for its new purchases of one million metric tons of wheat than would have been necessary had the wheat been purchased on the commercial market.[108]

Since 1 July 1994, the United States has subsidized the PRC's purchase of 3 million metric tons of wheat and has agreed to finance additional amounts after China exhausted that consignment. The U.S. Agriculture Department is authorized to spend a maximum of $800 million in funds from fiscal year 1995 to help U.S. farms compete with foreign grain producers. President Clinton's budget for fiscal year 1996 proposes $959 million to subsidize American grain exports.[109]

Concurrent with the IPR negotiations—on 18 February 1995—Energy Secretary Hazel R. O'Leary visited Beijing to negotiate PRC purchases of American-made electric-power systems. Secretary O'Leary's delegation comprised eighty officials and businessmen, representing sixty-five U.S. energy corporations. During its visit to Shanghai, the U.S.

delegation signed eight cooperative agreements exceeding $2 billion U.S. worth.[110]

In an article dated 7 February 1995, *New York Times* correspondent David E. Sanger wrote that Secretary O'Leary was to convey a message from Secretary of State Warren Christopher. Secretary Christopher sought the initiation of regular discussions on Chinese missile exports; as a *quid pro quo* for a full accounting of past sales, the United States would offer to forgive past violations.[111]

Through the strenuous efforts of the Departments of Commerce, Defense, and Treasury, Sino-American cooperation continues. Its expansion, however, is hindered by the absence of a concurrence on political and regional security matters. This inadequacy was identified on 26 July 1995 by Karen Elliot House, the president of Dow Jones International. Writing in *The Wall Street Journal,* Ms. House called for a strategic dialogue to match the $48 billion bilateral trade relationship.[112]

One of the impediments to Sino-American strategic cooperation is the question of Taiwan's identity. Another impediment to entente is the question of human rights. To appreciate the human-rights quandary in which China's leadership finds itself, and the exhaustive attempts that have been put forth by the United States to resolve the human-rights question, it behooves us to consider the current history of China's and America's human-rights policies.

Notes

1. Patrick E. Tyler, "As Deng Fades, China's Leaders Tighten Grip on Power," *New York Times,* 19 December 1994, p. A–3.

2. Elaine Sciolino, "Beijing Rebuffs U.S. on Halting Iran Atom Deal," *New York Times,* 18 April 1995, p. A–8.

3. William J. Clinton, "Report to Congress Concerning Extension of Waiver Authority for the People's Republic of China," 28 May 1993, *Public Papers of the Presidents of the United States,* p. 771.

4. "Executive Order: Conditions for Renewal of Most Favored Nation Status for the People's Republic of China in 1994," The White House, Office of the Press Secretary, 28 May 1993., p. 2.

5. William J. Clinton, *Report to Congress Concerning Extension of Waiver Authority for the People's Republic of China,* 8 June 1994, p. 2.

6. Elaine Sciolino, "Clinton and China: How Promise Self-Destructed," *New York Times,* 29 May 1994, p. 8; Senator Max Baucus, "A Strategy for Human Rights in China," 25 March 1994, p. 2; Executive Order, op. cit., pp. 1, 2.

7. Fewsmith, op. cit., p. 251; Patrick E. Tyler, "Rights in China Improve, Envoy Says," *New York Times,* 1 January 1994, p. 5.

8. Zweig, op. cit., p. 247; Harding, op. cit., pp. 99, 131.

9. Harding, op. cit., pp. 146, 147.

10. Ibid., p. 95.

11. Spero, op. cit., p. 123.

12. Dennis A. Rondinelli, *Expanding Sino-American Business and Trade* (London: Quorum Books, 1994), p. 78.

13. Elaine Sciolino, "Clinton and Chin: How Promise Self-Destructed," *New York Times,* 29 May 1994, p. 8.

14. Senator Max Baucus, "China Policy in the Age of Pacific Community," remarks of Senator Max Baucus to the U.S.–China Business Council, 19 January 1995, pp. 1, 2.

15. Elaine Sciolino, "In a Box: In China, Not Quite a Year after a Trade Compromise, Human Rights Issues Fester," *New York Times,* 16 January 1994, p. IV–2.

16. This delegation also included Representatives Norm Dicks (Washington), George Miller (California), Mike Synar (Oklahoma), Chet Edwards (Texas), and Rosa DeLauro of Connecticut. Patrick E. Tyler, "China Promises U.S. to Try to Improve Its Human Rights," *New York Times,* 16 January 1994, pp. 1, 9.

17. Thomas L. Friedman, "Bentsen Says China Isn't Doing Enough on Rights," *New York Times,* 20 January 1994, p. A–6.

18. Thomas L. Friedman, "U.S. and China Widen Accords on Civil Rights," *New York Times,* 21 January 1994, p. A–9; William J.

92

Clinton, *Report to Congress Concerning Extension of Waiver Authority for the People's Republic of China,* 8 June 1994, p. 10; Barbara Crossette, "China Signs Agreement with U.S. to Cut Exports Made by Prisoners," *New York Times,* 8 August 1992, p. 3; and David Zweig, op. cit., p. 247.

19. Rondinelli, op. cit., pp. 85–86.
20. The new understanding (of 20 January 1994) had three primary points. They are: (1) the PRC's regular and timely reports when the United States requests information about the possible use of prisoners to make products for exports; (2) increased frequency in the number of prison visits by U.S. customs officials; and (3) the submission by the U.S. of regular and timely reports to China regarding any such prison visits so Beijing will know what violations, if any, are discovered. Thomas L. Friedman, "U.S. and China Widen Accords on Civil Rights," *New York Times,* 21 January 1994, p. A–1; Rondinelli, op. cit., pp. 85– 86.
21. Thomas L. Friedman, "U.S. and China Widen Accords on Civil Rights," *New York Times,* 21 January 1994, p. A–9; William J. Clinton, *Report to Congress Concerning Extension of Waiver Authority for the People's Republic of China,* 8 June 1994, p. 10.
22. "Bentsen Cochairs Joint Economic Committee Meeting," *FBIS-China,* 21 January 1994, pp. 4–6.
23. Harris, op. cit., p. 271; William J. Clinton, *Report to Congress Concerning Extension of Waiver Authority for the People's Republic of China,* 8 June 1994, p. 11.
24. Thomas L. Friedman, "Bentsen Says China Isn't Doing Enough on Rights," *New York Times,* 20 January 1994, p. A–6; Patrick E. Tyler, "Crossroads for China: With Democratic Stirrings Among Chinese, U.S. Is Pressing Beijing on Crucial Choices," *New York Times,* 29 January 1994, p. 4.
25. Thomas L. Friedman, "Deal with China Urged By Bentsen," *New York Times,* 20 March 1994, p. 20.
26. Patrick E. Tyler, "Rights in China Improve, Envoy Says," *New York Times,* 1 January 1994, p. 5.
27. Winston Lord, Assistant Secretary for East Asian and Pacific Affairs, "Mid-Term Review of Most-Favored-Nation Status for China: Statement before the Subcommittee on Trade of the House Ways and Means Committee, Washington, D.C., February 24, 1994," *U.S. Department of State Dispatch,* 7 March 1994, Vol. 5, No. 10, pp. 127, 130; Patrick E. Tyler, "China: Slower Growth, Still

Spectacular," *New York Times*, 3 January 1994, p. C-9; Elaine Sciolino, "A Draft State Dept. Report Finds China's Rights Record Is Still Poor," *New York Times*, 12 January 1994, p. A–1.

28. Patrick E. Tyler, "Highest U.S. Rights Official Meets with Leading Chinese Dissident," *New York Times*, 28 February 1994, p. A–2.

29. Patrick E. Tyler, "Crossroads for China: With Democratic Stirrings among Chinese, U.S. Is Pressing Beijing on Crucial Choices," *New York Times*, 29 January 1994, p. 4; and Patrick E. Tyler, "China Promises U.S. to Try to Improve Its Human Rights," *New York Times*, 16 January 1994, pp. 1, 9.

30. "China Releases 3 Prisoners in Gesture to U.S.," *New York Times*, 5 February 1994, p. 4.

31. "U.S. Secretary of State Meets PRC Leaders," *FBIS-China*, 14 March 1994, p. 4.

32. William J. Clinton, *Report to Congress Concerning Extension of Waiver Authority for the People's Republic of China*, 8 June 1994, pp. 4, 5; and Elaine Sciolino, "Christopher Ends Beijing Talks Citing Modest Gains," *New York Times*, 14 March 1994, p. A–3.

33. Joseph Fewsmith, "America and China: Back from the Brink," *Current History*, Vol. 93, No. 584 (September 1994), p. 254; Patrick E. Tyler, "China Dissident, Hoping to Meet Christopher, Is Detained at Home," *New York Times*, 13 March 1994, p. 8.

34. Steven Greenhouse, "President Condemns Beijing; Christopher Visit Questioned," *New York Times*, 5 March 1994, p. 4; and Elaine Sciolino, "China Rejects Call from Christopher for Rights Gains," *New York Times*, 13 March 1994, p. 1.

35. Elaine Sciolino, "Sourly, Christopher's talks in Beijing Come to an End," *New York Times*, 15 March 1994, p. A–3; "Qian Qichen Discusses Sino-U.S. Relations," *FBIS-China*, 15 March 1994, p. 7.

36. Patrick E. Tyler, "Beijing Says It Could Live Well Even If U.S. Trade Was Cut Off," *New York Times*, 21 March 1994, p. A–1.

37. Rondinelli, op. cit., p. 8

38. Patrick E. Tyler, "Chinese Puzzle: After Months of Dialogue on Human Rights, Beijing Takes Harder Line toward the U.S.," *New York Times*, 14 March 1994, p. A–3.

39. Ibid., p. A–1.

40. Elaine Sciolino, "Clinton and China: How Promise Self-Destructed," *New York Times*, 29 May 1994, p. 8; and Patrick E. Tyler, "China Sees Risk to Its Stability in U.S. Demands," *New York Times*, 19 My 1994, p. A–1.

41. William J. Clinton, *Report to Congress Concerning Extension of Waiver Authority for the People's Republic of China,* 8 June 1994, p. 5.

42. William J. Clinton, "The President's News Conference of 26 May 1994," *Weekly Compilation of Presidential Documents,* Vol. 30, No. 21 (30 May 1994), pp. 1,166, 1,167.

43. Douglas Jehl, "U.S. Is to Maintain Trade Privileges for China's Goods: A Policy Reversal," *New York Times,* 27 May 1994, pp. A–1, A–8.

44. Patrick E. Tyler, "China Welcomes U.S. Trade Policy," *New York Times,* 28 May 1994, p. 5; and "Beijing Praises Decision," *New York Times,* 27 May 1994, p. A–8.

45. "U.S. Urged to Shift China Policy on Trade," *New York Times,* 30 January 1994, p. 3; Thomas L. Friedman, "U.S. May Ease Rights goals with Beijing," *New York Times,* 24 March 1994, p. A–1; and Douglas Jehl, "Clinton Stresses China Rights Goal," *New York Times,* 25 March 1994, p. A–12.

46. Steven Greenhouse, "Aide Says U.S. May Scrap an Across-the-Board Penalty for China," *New York Times,* 30 March 1994, p. A–10.

47. Patrick E. Tyler, "Beijing Is Warning Leading Dissident," *New York Times,* 27 February 1994, p. 4.

48. Patrick E. Tyler, "China Allows a Prominent Dissident to Leave," *New York Times,* 11 May 1994, p. A–12; and Patrick E. Tyler, "In a Surprise Gesture, China Releases a Major Dissident," *New York Times,* 14 May 1994, p. 7.

49. Thomas L. Friedman, "China May Allow U.S. Broadcasts," *New York Times,* 18 May 1994, p. A–1.

50. Douglas Jehl, "Clinton Makes No Progress with Beijing," *New York Times,* 3 May 1994, p. A–8; and Patrick E. Tyler, "Discontent Mounts in China, Shaking the Leaders," *New York Times,* 10 April 1994, p. 3.

51. Elaine Sciolino, "White House Gets Progress Report on Rights in China," *New York Times,* 24 May 1994, pp. A–1, A–6.

52. William J. Clinton, "The President's News Conference of 26 May 1994," *Weekly Compilation of Presidential Documents,* Vol. 30, No. 21 (30 May 1994), p. 1,168.

53. Thomas L. Friedman, "Democrats Press for a Compromise on Chinese Trade," *New York Times,* 21 April 1994, p. A–1; and Steven Greenhouse, "Aide Says U.S. May Scrap an Across-the-Board Penalty for China," *New York Times,* 30 March 1994, p. A–10.

54. Senator Max Baucus, "Where We Stand and Where We Go from Here: China Policy in 1994 and Beyond," Remarks of Senator Max Baucus to the U.S.–China Business Council, 27 January 1994, p. 5; and Thomas L. Friedman, "Senator Asks End to Threats Against China," *New York Times*, 27 January 1994, p. A–11.
55. Congressman Lee H. Hamilton, "The United States and China: Toward a Policy of Realism," Remarks to the American Enterprise Institute, 10 May 1994, p. 4.
56. Senator Bill Bradley, "Floor Statement by Senator Bill Bradley on China's Most Favored Nation Status," 18 May 1994, pp. 1, 2.
57. Bill Bradley, "Trade, the Real Engine of Democracy," *New York Times*, 25 May 1994, p. A–21; Thomas L. Friedman, "Legislator Urges Diplomacy to Improve Rights in China," *New York Times*, 11 May 994, p. A–12; and Elaine Sciolino, "Conflicting Pressures on Clinton Mount over China's Trade Status," *New York Times*, 20 May 1994, p. A–9.
58. Samuel R. Berger, "Most-Favored-Nation for China," *Good Morning America*, 27 May 1994 (Show #2075): p. 2; Elaine Sciolino, "Winston Lord: Where the Buck Stops on China and Human Rights," *New York Times*, 27 March 1994, p. 8.
59. Keith Bradsher, "Bill to Restrict China's Imports Loses in House," *New York Times*, 10 August 1994, p. A–7.
60. Edward A. Gargan, "Gauging the Consequences of Spurning China," *New York Times*, 21 March 1994, p. D–1; Catherine S. Manegold, "A.F.L.-C.I.O. Leader Urges End to China's Current Trade Status," *New York Times*, 14 April 1994, p. A–6; Rondinelli, op. cit., p. 11.
61. Lillian Craig Harris, op. cit., p. 201.
62. Dennis A. Rondinelli, op. cit., pp. 12, 13.
63. Business Coalition for U.S.–China Trade, *Importance of the Long-Term U.S.-China Commercial and Strategic Relationship*, p. 1; Rondinelli, op. cit., p. 17.
64. Edward A. Gargan, "Gauging the Consequences of Spurning China," *New York Times*, 21 March 1994, p. D–5.
65. Dennis A. Rondinelli, op. cit., p. 14; David Zweig, op. cit., pp. 250, 251.
66. Harry Harding, op. cit., p. 58.
67. Edward A. Gargan, "Gauging the Consequences of Spurning China," *New York Times*, 21 March 1994, p. D–5.
68. Rondinelli, op. cit., pp. 17, 18.

69. Edward A. Gargan, "Gauging the Consequences of Spurning China," *New York Times*, 21 March 1994, p. D–5; and Patrick E. Tyler, "Beijing Says It Could Live Well Even If U.S. Trade Was Cut Off" *New York Times*, 21 March 1994, pp. A-1, A–10.

70. Edward A. Gargan, "Gauging the Consequences of Spurning China," *New York Times*, 21 March 1994, pp. D–1, D–5.

71. Ferdinand Protzman, "Deals Offset Debate on China in Germany," *New York Times*, 6 July 1994, p. D–6; and "China Makes Trade Pleas," *New York Times*, 12 September 1994, p. D–4; and Matt Marshall, "German Chinese Deals Ringing Hollow," *The Wall Street Journal*, 14 July 1995, p. A–8.

72. Patrick E. Tyler, "Awe-Struck U.S. Executives Survey the China Market," *New York Times*, 2 September 1994, p. D–2.

73. Ferdinand Protzman, "Deals Offset Debate on China in Germany," *New York Times*, 6 July 1994, p. D–6.

74. David Zweig, op. cit., p. 247.

75. Joan E. Spero, op. cit., p. 124.

76. "Secretary Brown's Mission to China Leads to Breakthrough in Trade," *Business America*, October 1994, p. 29; and Patrick E. Tyler, "China Agrees to Resume Talks with U.S. on Human Rights," *New York Times*, 31 August 1994, p. A–2; Tyler, "Awe-Struck U.S. Executives Survey the China Market," *New York Times*, 2 September 1994, p. D1961.

77. On 30 August 1994, Secretary Brown announced a Chinese commitment to reinvigorate a high-level Sino-American discussion on human rights. Specifically, concurrent meetings were to transpire in Washington and in New York at the end of September. Qian Qichen—the PRC Foreign Minister—was to meet with Secretary of State Christopher in Washington. John Shattuck—the Assistant Secretary of State for Democracy, Human Rights and Labor—was to meet with a PRC Foreign Ministry functionary in New York; Patrick E. Tyler, "Sidetracking Rights, U.S. Aide Pursues Business in China," *New York Times*, 30 August 1994, p. A–6; and Patrick E. Tyler, "China Agrees to Resume Talks with U.S. on Human Rights," *New York Times*, 31 August 1994, p. A–2.

78. "Wu, Brown Sign Landmark Accord to Expand Commercial Ties," *FBIS-China*, 30 August 1994, p. 6.

79. During the delegation's visit to Shanghai, Secretary Brown met with Wu Bangguo—the Secretary of the Shanghai Committee of the CCP—to learn of Shanghai's reforms; and "Shanghai, U.S. Sign

Electric Agreement," *FBIS-China,* 2 September 1994, p. 33; and "Official: U.S. Must Lift Sanctions to Open Market," *FBIS-China,* 1 September 1994, pp. 5, 6.

80. "Wu, Brown Sign Landmark Accord to Expand Commercial Ties," *FBIS-China,* 30 August 1994, p. 6.

81. "Secretary Brown's Mission to China Leads to Breakthrough in Trade," *Business America,* October 1994, p. 30.

82. "Wu, Brown Sign Landmark Accord to Expand Commercial Ties," *FBIS-China,* 30 August 1994, pp. 6, 7; and "Media Commentary on Commerce Secretary Brown's Visit," *FBIS-China,* 1 September 1994, p. 7.

83. "Secretary Brown's Mission to China Leads to Breakthrough in Trade," *Business America,* October 1994, pp. 56, 57.

84. "China Makes Trade Pleas," *New York Times,* 12 September 1994, p. D–4; "Official: U.S. Must Lift Sanctions to Open Market," *FBIS-China,* 1 September 1994, pp. 5, 6.

85. Elaine Sciolino, "U.S. Moves to Ease Beijing Sanctions," *New York Times,* 8 March 1994, p. A–8.

86. "Liu Huaqing Meets U.S. Under Secretary of Defense," *FBIS-China,* 15 March 1994, p. 9.

87. Elaine Sciolino, "China Trip Begins on a Frosty Note for Christopher," *New York Times,* 12 March 1994, p. 4; and Sciolino, "U.S. Showing Frustration Over China's Human Rights Policy," *New York Times,* 9 March 1994, p. A–11.

88. "U.S. Defense Secretary Perry Arrives in Beijing," *FBIS-China,* 17 October 1994, pp. 11–13.

89. Michael R. Gordon, "Perry Visit Seeks to Rebuild Ties with Chinese Military," *New York Times,* 17 October 1994, p. A–8.

90. "Foreign Ministry Holds Weekly News Conference: Spokesman Comments on Perry Visit," *FBIS-China,* 20 October 1994, p. 1.

91. "Liu Huaqing, Perry hold 'Friendly' Talks," *FBIS-China,* 18 October 1994, pp. 5, 6.

92. Michael R. Gordon, "U.S. to China: Be More Open on Arms Plan," *New York Times,* 19 October 1994, p. A–14.

93. "Communications Satellites: The Long March Back to China," *The Economist,* 5 November 1994, p. 67.

94. Marcus W. Brauchli, "Imposition of Trade Sanctions Exposes a Contradictory U.S. Approach to China," *Wall Street Journal,* 7 February 1995, p. A–19; and David E. Sanger, "President Imposes

Trade Sanctions on Chinese Goods," *New York Times,* 5 February 1995, p. 12.

95. David E. Sanger, "U.S. Threatens $2.8 Billion of Tariffs on China Exports," *New York Times,* 1 January 1995, p. 14; "China Warns It Will Retaliate If U.S. Proceeds With Sanctions," *New York Times,* 1 January 1995, p. 14.

96. David E. Rosenbaum, "China Trade Rift with U.S. Deepens," *New York Times,* 29 January 1995, p. 1.

97. David E. Rosenbaum, "China Trade Rift with U.S. Deepens," *New York Times,* 29 January 1995, p. 8; and Sen. Max Baucus, "China Policy in the Age of Pacific Community," remarks of Sen. Max Baucus to the U.S.–China Business Council, 19 January 1995, p. 6.

98. Rosenbaum, op. cit., p. 8.

99. Craig S. Smith, "Major Firms in U.S.-China trade Say Sanctions by U.S. Wouldn't Hurt Much," *Wall Street Journal,* 7 February 1995, pp. A–2, A–12; and David E. Sanger, "President Imposes Trade Sanctions on Chinese Goods," *New York Times,* 5 February 1995, p. 1.

100. Helene Cooper and Robert S. Greenberger, "U.S. and China Agree to Meet Next Week in Fresh Attempt to Avert a Trade War," *Wall Street Journal,* 7 February 1995, p A–2.

101. David E. Sanger, "President Imposes Trade Sanctions on Chinese Goods," *New York Times,* 5 February 1995, p. 12; and Craig S. Smith, "Major Firms in U.S.-China Trade Say Sanctions by U.S. Wouldn't Hurt Much," *Wall Street Journal,* 7 February 1995, p. A–12.

102. Craig S. Smith, op. cit., p. A–2; David E. Sanger, op. cit., p. 12; and Sanger, "Chinese Invite U.S. to Resume Talks on Trade," *New York Times,* 7 February 1995, p. D–6; and Sanger, "This Is a Trade War! Get Your Popgun!" *New York Times,* 12 February 1995, p. IV–1; and Steven Mufson, "China Says Crackdown on CD Pirates Widens," *Washington Post,* 16 February 1995, p. A–34.

103. Seth Faison, "U.S. And China Sign Accord to End Piracy of Software, Music Recordings and Film," *New York Times,* 27 February 1995, pp. A–1, D–6; and David Cay Johnston, "Cautious Praise for Pact from U.S. Business," *New York Times,* 27 February 1995, pp. D–1, D–6.

104. David E. Sanger, "In a Trade Pack with China, a Ghost of Japan," *New York Times,* 27 February 1995, p. D–6.

99

105. Helene Cooper and Robert S. Greenberger, "U.S. and China Agree to Meet Next Week in Fresh Attempt to Avert a Trade War," *Wall Street Journal,* 7 February 1995, p. A–12.
106. Seth Faison, "China Closes a Disk Factory as Sanctions Deadline Nears," *New York Times,* 26 February 1995, p. 6; and Martha M. Hamilton & Steven Mufson, "Clinton Hails Accord with China on Trade," *Washington Post,* 27 February 1995, p. A–16; and Steven Mufson, "China Says Crackdown on CD Pirates Widens," *Washington Post,* 16 February 1995, p. A–34.
107. Patrick E. Tyler, "New Dispute Imperils Trade with Chinese," *New York Times,* 12 March 1995, p. 21.
108. David E. Sanger, "Trade Fight Aside, U.S. to Sell China More Wheat," *New York Times,* 8 February 1995, p. D–1.
109. David E. Sanger, "Trade Fight Aside, U.S. to Sell China More Wheat," *New York Times,* 8 February 1995, p. D–18.
110. "Energy Secretary O'Leary's Trip to China," *FBIS-China,* 21 February 1995, pp. 2–5.
111. David E. Sanger, "Chinese Invite U.S. to Resume Talks on Trade," *New York Times,* 7 February 1995, p. D–6.
112. Karen Elliot House, "Drifting toward Disaster in Asia," *The Wall Street Journal,* 26 July 1995, p. A–12.

III / China, America, and the Question of Human Rights

The PRC's Post-Tiananmen Policies on Human Rights

The question of human rights in China—and how to effectively approach it—has heavily influenced the careers of top Chinese leaders throughout their nation's recent history. On 16 January 1987, Hu Yao-bang—who had served as General Secretary of the Chinese Communist Party (CCP) since 1982—resigned largely because of his failed efforts at democratic reform. And on 24 June 1989, the career of Zhao Ziyang—Mr. Hu's successor as CCP General Secretary—was also abbreviated because of the human-rights-related disputes attending the Tiananmen Square massacre of 4 June.[1]

Mr. Bao Tong—who had served as political secretary to the Communist Party Politburo and as a top aide to the Prime Minister Zhao Ziyang—is another example. Mr. Bao was expelled from the party for opposing the 1989 crackdown on pro-democracy students, and was sentenced to a seven-year prison sentence on 21 July 1992.[2]

The importance that the Chinese leadership attaches to the human-rights question was revealed on 24 July 1994, in an article by *New York Times* correspondent Philip Shenon. In 1993, Beijing established an international lobbying group called the China Society for Human Rights Studies. Its founding president, Mr. Zhu Muzhi, oversees a budget approximating $120,000, which is primarily underwritten by donations from state-owned companies. Zhu Muzhi, age eighty, formerly served as director of the official New China News Agency. In June 1994, the Human Rights Society released a twenty-one-page booklet to rebut the State Department's 1994 report on human rights in China.[3]

On 21 August 1993—to contend with the continuing clamor for democratic reform—PRC President Jiang Zemin opened an anticorruption drive. President Jiang did so through a keynote address at the second meeting of the Second Plenary Session of the CCP Central Committee Discipline Inspection Commission. President Jiang—who is also the Chinese Communist Party's General Secretary—delivered his speech at Beijing's Great Hall of the People. As *New York Times* correspondent Nicholas D. Kristof reported on 22 August, 1993, this widespread dissatisfaction contributed directly toward the 1989 Tiananmen democracy movement protests.[4]

Popular concern was and is propelled by the arbitrary sentencing and detention policies that the Chinese government employs. The convening of the annual National People's Congress prompts the PRC police network to suppress dissidents. Just before the Eighth People's Congress convened on 10 March 1994, the Public Security Bureau detained such dissidents as Zhou Guoqiang, Qian Yumin, Bao Ge, Yuan Hongbin, and Wang Jiaqi.[5] The arrival of a foreign dignitary is often preceded by a campaign of mass arrests. Two examples are posited here.

On 5 March 1994—one week before Secretary of State Christopher's visit to Beijing—the PRC's public security authorities released Wei Jingsheng after rearresting and detaining him for one day. Wei Jingsheng is China's preeminent human-rights martyr. On 9 April 1994—just before the arrival of French Prime Minister Edouard Balladur, several Shanghai dissidents were detained. Their number included Bao Ge, Xu Wenli, and Wang Fuchen. Mr. Xu Wenli had been paroled after a lengthy prison term. Mr. Bao Ge—who advocates compensation for Chinese victims of Japanese wartime atrocities—was detained as well on 21 March 1994, during a visit by Japanese Prime Minister Morihiro Hosokawa.[6]

The Public Security Bureau prefers to detain its political and religious dissidents without a court trial. *New York Times* correspondent Steven Greenhouse wrote that only once—on 14 January 1994-has China released dissidents before they were tried. The two Tibetan dissidents—Gendun Rinchen and Lobsang Yonten—had been arrested in May 1993 for stealing state secrets.[7]

In its 1994 report on human rights in China, Amnesty International explained that this administrative detention is implemented under two programs: (1) "shelter and investigation"; and (2) "re-education through labor." Of the two, "re-education through labor" appears to be the program preferred by PRC authorities.

On 12 October 1994, *The New York Times* reported that at least three Shanghai dissidents have been sentenced to lengthy terms of "re-education through labor." The human-rights campaigners—Yang Qinheng, Yang Zhou, and Bao Ge—were reported to have been sentenced to three years. Yang Qinheng is a businessman. Yang Zhou, age fifty-one, is a founder of the Shanghai-based Association for Human Rights. On 15 July 1995, Yang Zhou was released on medical parole because of a throat tumor.[8] And as forementioned, Mr. Bao has irritated the PRC Public Security Bureau with his persistence in demanding compensation from Japan for Chinese victims of wartime atrocities.[9]

Although it theoretically holds a maximum penalty of three years, a sentence of "re-education through labor" can in practice be extended on a year-by-year basis. The 1995 report issued by the U.S. Department of State supported this assessment with detailed examples:

A number of religious activists remained imprisoned in 1994. There was some evidence that authorities have increasingly used short-term detentions, rather than long prison terms when dealing with unauthorized religious activists.[10]

An individual can be detained under the auspices of "re-education through labor" for such activities as: (1) contacting "anti-China overseas organizations"; (2) teaching in an unregistered Catholic seminary; or (3) meeting with a visiting U.S. Congressman or diplomat.[11]

Those dissidents who are sentenced can expect to be held for as long as three years. The year 1994 witnessed two examples. On 23 July 1994, *New York Times* correspondent Philip Shenon reported that a trial of fourteen dissidents—the first major political trial in Beijing since 1991—was coming to a close. Most of the dissidents had been arrested in May and June 1992. The trial—which was closed to the public—reportedly began on 14 July 1994, in Beijing's Intermediate Court.[12]

The second example occurred on 16 December 1994, when nine pro-democracy dissidents were sentenced. The dissidents had been detained in jail for thirty months. The heaviest sentence—that of twenty years—was received by Hu Shigen, a thirty-nine-year-old lecturer at the Beijing Languages Institute, for "spreading counter-revolutionary propaganda." The eight other dissidents were convicted on sentences ranging from three to twelve years. Five others were convicted and released, and one was placed "under surveillance" for two more years.[13]

On 29 January 1994, *New York Times* correspondent Patrick E. Tyler wrote that the People's Republic of China "has more than 1,200 prisons, labor camps and detention centers." Foreigners—including tourists from Taiwan and Hong Kong—are detainable if they proselytize for Christianity without authorization, but have been known to secure releases for a fee equivalent to $118 (i.e., 1,000 RenMinBi in Chinese currency).[14]

Citizens of the Chinese People's Republic, however, are not afforded such latitude. Amnesty International claims that those Beijing residents who were connected with the events surrounding the incident of 4 June 1989 were sent to serve their sentences in such places as: (1) Beijing Prison No. 2; (2) Hanyang Prison, in Hubei Province; (3) the Qinghe farm, a labor camp near Tianjin; (4) labor camps in the Hebei province; or (5) detention centers in the remote western region of Xinjiang.[15]

The State Department reported that "there were 2,678 people serving sentences for counterrevolutionary crimes at the end of 1994." This figure, while appalling, represents a steady decrease from the 2,935 prisoners counted in March of 1994 and the 3,172 cited in December of 1993. Political prisoners serving in Beijing prisons 1 and 2 receive the heaviest sentences, many of them life imprisonment.[16]

Hanyang Prison—known formally as the Hubei Provincial No. 1 Reform through Labour Detachment—is a labor camp covering several square kilometers. Its location—in the area of Wuhan, the provincial capital of Hubei—is in the city of Hanyang.[17]

The Qinghe farm—formally known as the Beijing No. 1 Reform though Labour Detachment—is described as a huge complex comprising agricultural units and factories.

Although the Qinghe farm is located in Chadian, between Beijing and Tianjin cities, it is operated by the municipal government of Beijing. Amnesty International reports that of the 500 prisoners initially assigned to this facility in 1989, "over 300 of these prisoners have by now been released." The same report provided a profile of the 171 prisoners who continue to serve sentences ranging from five to ten-years' imprisonment:

> Many of them are young people who were in their late teens or early 20s at the time of their arrest. They are held in different "sub-farms," or sections of the farm, namely in sections No. 3, No. 6 and No. 8. In each section, they are held in special squadrons, commonly referred to as the "ruffians' squadrons," which were especially established for the 1989 prisoners.[18]

The State Department report pointed out that these prison sentences directly and adversely affect the families of those imprisoned. The impact is acutely felt in connection with employment and housing prospects. The following example concerns the family of Ren Wanding, an accountant and an outspoken fifty-one-year-old human-rights martyr of the Cultural Revolution and the Democracy Wall movement:

> For example, Zhang Fengying, wife of imprisoned activist Ren Wanding, and her teenage daughter were evicted from their apartment, owned by Ren's work unit, in 1992 and remained in poor housing during 1994.[19]

The Human Faces of Human Rights

A comprehensive profile of each prominent PRC political prisoner would exceed the scope of this paper's pretensions. To more adequately comprehend the human rights situation in China, however, it might best behoove us to examine a few individual cases-in-point.

Wei Jingsheng

Wei Jingsheng, age forty-six, is China's preeminent dissident. He first achieved fame as a leader in the "Democracy Wall" movement of 1978. Mr. Wei—who was at the time an electrician at the Beijing Zoo—was sentenced to fifteen years of imprisonment in March of 1979, and was released on six-month's parole on 14 September 1993.[20] During his fourteen and a half years in prison, Mr. Wei spent years in solitary confinement, passed one nine-month period without being allowed to bathe, lost many of his teeth from malnutrition, and developed heart trouble. He was redetained on 1 April 1994, and has been held incommunicado since then.[21]

Mr. Wei was detained anew on 1 April 1994, for "violating his parole conditions." Two activities by Mr. Wei drew the attention of China's Public Security Bureau. The first activity concerned controversial correspondence. Mr. Wei sent a letter to the International Olympic Committee asking that body to impose sanctions against China for the PRC's decision to jail Qing Yongmin in November 1993. Qing Yongmin, a young pamphleteer, had opposed China's bid to play host to the 2000 Summer games.[22]

The second activity occurred on 27 February 1994, when Wei Jingsheng held an unauthorized meeting with

U.S. Assistant Secretary of State John Shattuck. Mr. Shattuck—who serves as Assistant Secretary of State for Democracy, Rights and Labor—is the State Department's top human-rights official.[23]

Within the first five months of his six-month parole period. Wei Jingsheng received at least seven warnings from the PRC Public Security Bureau. Then on April 1st—while he was en route to Beijing after a month of self-imposed exile from the capital—Mr. Wei's car was stopped. Chinese security agents—seven carloads of them—arrested Mr. Wei. He has not been seen since. Wei Jingsheng's secretary, Tong Yi, began serving a two-and-a-half a-year sentence of "reeducation through labor" in December 1994 for forgery of an official stamp. (Ms. Tong Yi had been detained since 6 April 1994.)[24]

On 30 March 1995, Chen Jian, a PRC Foreign Ministry spokesman, said that China would not respond to international appeals for the release of Wei Jingsheng. Mr. Chen characterized this question as a matter of "China's internal affairs."[25] Nearly eight months later—on 21 November 1995—Wei Jingsheng was formally charged with trying to "overthrow the Chinese government."[26]

Bao Tong

On 14 May 1994, the wife of Mr. Bao Tong, now age sixty-one, implored the international community to secure the release of her husband on medical grounds. Bao Tong was expelled from the party for opposing the 1989 crackdown on pro-democracy students. On 21 July 1992, a people's court sentenced Mr. Bao to seven years in prison. Prior to his expulsion, he had served as: (1) political secretary to the Communist Party Politburo; (2) the head of a

Party institute examining political reforms; and (3) as a top aide to Prime Minister Zhao Ziyang. Mr. Bao, who suffers from colon cancer, has received the attention of the United States Senate and the Clinton Administration. The PRC Ministry of Public Security holds Mr. Bao in solitary confinement, and has refused family pleas for information or private treatment.[27]

Chen Ziming

It is difficult to discuss Chen Ziming without discussing his former colleague, Wang Juntao. Messrs. Wang and Chen were concurrently arrested, and each received thirteen-year prison sentences on 12 February 1991 for fomenting the democracy movement in the 1980s.[28]

Like Chen Ziming, Mr. Wang—then a thirty-eight-year-old physics graduate from Beijing University—was a social scientist, a writer, and a political organizer. Wang Juntao and Chen Ziming were codirectors of the Beijing Social and Economic Sciences Research Institute, the newspaper of which—*Economics Weekly*—strongly advocated political reform and democracy before the 1989 crackdown.[29]

Like Chen Ziming, Mr. Wang was released on "medical parole" on 14 May 1994. Unlike Mr. Chen, Wang Juntao left China for treatment of hepatitis and heart treatment in New York in April of 1994. Chen Ziming refused to leave China, and remains a captive in his tiny apartment, where as many as fifty-six policemen over time have kept him under guard and heavy surveillance. Mr. Chen, now age forty-five, suffers from hepatitis, heart disease, and testicular cancer.[30]

On 4 June 1995, Chen Ziming issued an open letter demanding the release of political prisoners and the rehabilitation of the former Communist Party chief Zhao Ziyang.

109

He concurrently conducted a twenty-four-hour fast to cele-brate the sixth anniversary of the Tiananmen Square crack-down. Three weeks later—on 25 June—the PRC police took Mr. Chen into custody and revoked his medical parole.[31]

Fang Zheng

On 1 September 1994, Fang Zheng—China's national discus champion—was prevented from competing in the Far East and South Pacific Disabled Games. This competi-tion is China's Special Olympics for the disabled. Fang Zheng's current disqualification stems from the govern-ment's belated discovery that his legs were amputated after being crushed by a army tank during the 1989 military crackdown around Tiananmen Square.

Fang Zheng began training for the discus after losing his legs. In the Third National Disabled Games—held in Guangzhou in March 1992—he won two gold medals. At that time he participated as a member of the Beijing team.

Despite representations by Deng Pufang—China's most influential advocate for the disabled, and the eldest son of Deng Xiaoping—to the PRC Sports Ministry, Fang Zheng was not allowed to compete. Initially, Fang Zheng enjoyed the support of: (1) the China Welfare Fund for the Disabled, whose chairman is Deng Pufang; and (2) the China Disabled Persons Federations, directed by Liu Xiao-cheng. These sponsors—which receive large cash grants from state-owned Chinese companies—disavowed any connection with or sponsorship of Fang Zheng after 19 July 1994, when the PRC Sports Ministry expelled the discus champion from China's national team.[32]

Gao Yu

Ms. Gao is a prominent journalist who had been invited to Columbia University as a visiting scholar in 1994. She had written articles about the political maneuvering of China's leaders for Hong Kong–based magazines. In November 1994—after a closed trial—Ms. Gao was sentenced to six years' imprisonment for "leaking state secrets abroad." According to the State Department Report, Gao Yu's lawyer and her relatives were not notified of the final trial or sentencing; her case had been returned twice for insufficient evidence.[33]

Liu Gang

Liu Gang, now age thirty-three was a physics student, drawn into the orbit of the controversial Prof. Fang Lizhi. Mr. Liu was third on a list of twenty-one student leaders most wanted by the authorities after the Tiananmen demonstrations of May and June 1989. He was sentenced on 12 February 1991 to six years in prison for "conspiracy to subvert the Government."[34]

On 4 March 1994—in an attempt to show flexibility on human rights—five American journalists were taken on a tour of a nearly deserted Lingyuan No. 2 labor reform camp. Liu Gang was the focus of the prison visit. Amnesty International reported that "the journalists were able to see Liu Gang, through a glass panel, but were denied permission to talk to him." The report added that Mr. Liu's father and sister have been denied permission by the Lingyuan prison authorities to visit him. The State Department report claims that in February 1994, "a member of the China Human Rights Society, an organization established primarily to study and defend China's human rights record, was allowed to meet Liu and review his medical records in an attempt to refute reports that he had been mistreated."[35]

Mr. Liu—unlike his pro-democracy comrades Ren Wanding and Bao Tong—has since been released from prison. On 19 June 1995, *The New York Times* reported that Liu Gang had been freed from prison after completing a six-year prison term. Mr. Liu, however, is restricted to his home district for two years, cannot speak with foreign reporters, and must refrain from contact with "enemies of the state."[36]

Wang Dan

Wang Dan, age twenty-six, achieved recognition as a Beijing University student leader during the 1989 pro-democracy demonstrations. On 26 January 1991, Wang Dan was jailed for four years because of these activities. He remains under close police surveillance and suffers from occasional police harassment, making it difficult for him to live a normal life. Wang Dan was threatened physically in December 1994 by undercover police officers. Fearing physical harm, Wang disappeared from public view for 4 weeks before returning home. His home remains under close and heavy surveillance. On 22 May 1995, *The New York Times* reported that the PRC police had re-detained Wang Dan. Wang Dan has conducted several hunger strikes to protest this mistreatment.[37]

Xi Yang

On 27 September 1993, Xi Yang—a reporter for the

Ming Bao newspaper based in Hong Kong—was arrested for suspicious newsgatheirng. From that time until his closed trial in March 1994, Mr. Xi had been denied access to his family and an independent legal counsel. Xi Yang was sentenced to twelve years' imprisonment and two years' deprivation of political rights. His crime—"spying and stealing state secrets"—concerned classified information on China's strategies for: (1) the sale of gold; and (2) interest rates. Xi Yang's activity is alleged to have been aided and abetted by Tian Ye, a bank official who was convicted for delivering the data. Mr. Tian was sentenced to fifteen years' imprisonment and three years' deprivation of political rights.[38]

Xu Liangying

Dr. Xu Liangying, age seventy-five, was a historian at the Academy of Sciences. Mr. Xu had helped to translate Albert Einstein's collected works into Chinese. Dr. Xu's contribution to China's human-rights campaign, however, has been the organization of other dissidents to petition the government for democratic reforms.[39]

On 10 March 1994—under Dr. Xu Liangying's leadership—a total of seven leading Chinese scientists and intellectuals appealed to PRC President Jiang Zemin for an end to the repression of free speech and for the release of all political prisoners. The six signatories joining Dr. Xu were: Ding Zilin and Jian Peikun, philosophy professors whose son was killed during the 1989 military crackdown; Shao Yanxiang, a poet; Zhang Kangkang, a writer; Liu Liao, a physicist; and historian Wang Laili, Professor Xu's wife. The appeal concurred with the opening session of the National People's Congress, and preceded by a day Secretary of

State Warren Christopher's arrival in Beijing on 11 March 1994. It also followed Wei Jingsheng's detention, after he had met on 27 February 1994 with U.S. Assistant Secretary of State John Shattuck.[40]

Dr. Xu's activity was not unprecedented; petitions have preceded and postdated his March missive. On 26 January 1994, eleven dissidents signed a two-page statement calling for the release of Qin Yongmin, a young pamphleteer sentenced in December 1993 by the Public Security Bureau to two years of hard labor. Qin Yongmin's crime had urged nonviolent political change in a "peace charter" that was drafted by nine Beijing dissidents in November of 1993.[41]

Several subsequent efforts followed in the first half of 1995. On 25 February 1995, 12 prominent intellectuals formally petitioned the PRC's parliamentary bodies to investigate corruption in the Chinese leadership. This document demanded an independent judiciary and constitutional democracy as well. The petition—a 2,000-word document—was delivered to the National People's Congress and the Chinese People's Political Consultative Conference.[42]

The signatories included: Wang Ruoshui and Wu Xuecan, both of whom had formerly served as *People's Daily* editors; Chen Ziming; Xu Wenli, a close friend of Wei Jingsheng; Bao Zunxin, a former editor of the respected *Reading* magazine; Liu Xiao Bo, a writer critical of CCP abuses against personal liberties; and Min Qi, the former editor of *Chinese Social Sciences* magazine.[43]

On March 1995—in their second petition in less than a week—the same twelve intellectuals called for greater control of indiscriminate police powers. Specifically, the petition requested that the PRC Parliament rescind the powers of Prime Minister Li Peng, regarding unconstitutional arrest procedures that allow the police to detain as many as 1 million Chinese annually.

The second petition was presented immediately before the opening of the National People's Congress, which convened on March 5th. Its signatories were the same as those on the first one. In addition to the forementioned names, the signers included: Chen Xiaoping, a constitutional scholar; a sociologist, Zhuo Duo; a poet, Liao Yiwu; a magazine editor, Jin Cheng; and a pro-democracy advocate, Sha Yuguang.[44]

Sandwiched between these two twelve-dissident petitions was a separate signing campaign. This effort was led by former student leader Wang Dan, and was endorsed by twenty five other pro-democracy advocates. It produced a letter that comprised two demands: (1) an improvement in respect to human rights conditions; and (2) an end to one-party rule.[45]

On 15 May 1995, forty-five scientists and intellectuals presented a petition to the Chinese leadership, requesting a reversal of the verdict imposed upon those who participated in the pro-democracy movement preceding the massacre of 4 June 1989. The most prominent petitioner—Wang Ganchang, age eighty-eight—is one of China's premier nuclear physicists, and is the designer of China's first atomic bomb.[46]

These efforts have yet to elicit the desired official response. On 4 March 1995, Zhou Jue—the spokesman for the National People's Congress—reportedly said that the Government would ignore the petitions.[47] As detailed in the State Department Report, organized opposition to the Chinese Communist Party is simply not tolerated:

The requirement that associations register and be approved makes it difficult for independent interest groups to form and affect the system.[48]

This is especially true in respect to workers' rights. In March 1994, Liu Nianchun was disallowed from registering the Association for the Protection of Labor Rights. His endeavour resulted in a detention (without formal criminal charge) of five months, from May to October. On 22 May 1995, *The New York Times* reported that the PRC police had re-detained Liu Nianchun.[49]

Likewise, labor leader Han Dongfang cannot return to China, because the Chinese Government has cancelled his passport and thereby rendered him a stateless person. This decision violates three provisions of the Universal Declaration on Human Rights. Article 9 of the Universal Declaration states that "no one shall be subjected to arbitrary arrest, detention or exile." Article 13, paragraph 2, states that "everyone has the right to leave any country including his own, and to return to his country." Article 15 states that "no one shall be arbitrarily deprived of his nationality nor denied the right to change his nationality."[50]

Another labor activist, Zhou Guoqiang, was sentenced in September 1994 to three years of "re-education through labor." Mr. Zhou's "crime" was the advocacy of workers' rights at the National People's Congress in March of 1994. In addition to sale of politically oriented T-shirts at the National People's Congress, Mr. Zhou—along with fellow attorney Yuan Hongbing—petitioned for: (1) the right to strike; and (2) the right to organize non-official trade unions.[51]

Two recent confrontations clarify that the Chinese intellectual community cannot effectively protest or challenge their government. On 18 May 1995, Liu Xiaobo was arrested by the Beijing Public Security Bureau as he pre-

116

pared to issue a 56-signature petition to the government commemorating the casualties of the 1989 crackdown. Liu Xiaobo, age forty, is a literary scholar and critic. His arrest took place as he was preparing to deliver the petition to a Western news organization.[52]

The second confrontation was exposed on 28 May 1995, when *The New York Times* reported that the PRC police had detained twenty-two additional dissidents. This detention was part of a crackdown extending from Hangzhou to Nanjing in eastern China, to Xian in the northwest and Chongqing in the southwest. One of the five dissidents apprehended in Hangzhou on 24 May, Lin Mu had served as an aide to Hu Yaobang, the former General Secretary of the Communist Party. Hu Yaobang's death—on 15 April 1989—catalyzed the Tiananmen Square pro-democracy demonstrations.[53]

Upon whom, then, has the responsibility for human-rights advocacy devolved?

Harry Wu

One outspoken and effective critic of China's human rights repression, Mr. Harry Wu, is a Chinese who naturalized to American citizenship. Mr. Wu is fifty-eight years of age. Mr. Wu's field research has provided the basis for: (1) a BBC documentary on China's organ trade; and (2) a decision by the U.S. Customs Service to impose a ban on the importation of two dozen Chinese products.[54] On 19 July 1995, Mr. Wu was detained at outpost of Horgas, on the Chinese border with Kazakhstan. On 8 July—in Wuhan—he was formally charged with: (1) spying; (2) theft of state secrets; and (3) "sneaking" into the country. Mr. Wu had previously spent 19 years in labor camps before immigrating to the United States. These charges have been upheld despite the fact that Mr. Wu was carrying a valid passport and visa.[55] No United States diplomat had been allowed to visit Mr. Wu until Arturo Macies—the U.S. Consul General in Beijing—visited him in his native Wuhan on 10 July; a second visit—this one by U.S. Consul Daniel Piccuta—followed on 9 August. Amplifying his humiliation was a thirteen-minute videotape, which was released on 27 July, in which Mr. Wu allegedly recants his previous human-rights activities. The videotape—entitled "Just See the Lies of Wu Hongda"—was filmed by the PRC police. On 24 August, Mr. Wu was sentenced to fifteen years in prison and ordered expelled from the country. Although he has since returned to the United States, he vows to return to China to bring attention to the as-yet-unresolved human-rights dilemma in China.[56]

Only the government of the United States of America has the diplomatic and financial stature to effectively confront the Chinese leadership on this moral question. As Secretary of State Christopher explained in his speech to the National Press Club on 28 July:

> On human rights issues, every nation must find its own way, consistent with its history and culture. But at the same time, all have a responsibility to meet international obligations and to respect the standards of the Universal Declaration of Human Rights. America will continue to champion human rights in the movement toward open societies and will do so without arrogance but also without apologies.[57]

The author's chauvinistic attitude notwithstanding, it behooves the reader to briefly consider the current American diplomatic efforts toward the question of China's human rights.

U.S. Diplomacy toward the Question of Human Rights in China

Since the suppression of the 1989 democracy demonstrations by the People's Liberation Army on 3 and 4 June, American negotiators have worked at a disadvantage. The desire of a citizen to permanently leave his nation represents a tremendous embarrassment to that nation's government. This truth applies to all countries. As Dr. James V. Feinerman—a law professor at Georgetown University—explained in the September 1990 issue of *Current History,* this universal truth obtains especially in China:

> Although the public security dragnet aided the arrest of several of the most wanted fugitives, the Chinese government was greatly embarrassed by the escape to the West of leaders like Wuer Kaixi, Yan Jiaqi and Chai Ling.[58]

When President Clinton made his Most-Favored-Nation decision on 27 May 1994, many believed that China's dissidents would soon be freed and that the People's Republic would move smartly to remove the human rights obstacles that had been in place since 1989. But on 29 August 1994, *New York Times* correspondent Patrick E. Tyler wrote that China's leadership had taken a number of actions contradictory to earlier pledges of cooperation.[59] Specifically, China indefinitely postponed discussions with the International Committee of the Red Cross to open prisons as a means of checking reports of torture and political detention. China also severed discussions with the Voice of America on ending the jamming of some broadcasts. And China continued and intensified its arrest of religious, labor and democracy advocates.[60]

America and the industrialized democracies continue

to be disappointed with the inflexibility of China's policy on human rights. On 16 January 1995—after two and one-half days of meetings with *inter alios,* Vice Foreign Minister Liu Huaqiu—Assistant Secretary of State John Shattuck announced that no progress had been made in terms of freedom of speech, association and religion. Theretofore, the high-level Sino-American dialogue on human rights had been dormant. This January visit was Mr. Shattuck's first return to China since 27 February 1994, at which time transpired his controversial meeting with dissident Wei Jingsheng.[61]

In March, Sino-American confrontations continued in both bilateral and multilateral fora. On 1 March 1995—in what *New York Times* correspondent Patrick E. Tyler termed "a blunt diplomatic exchange," Chinese Foreign Minister Qian Qichen asked Assistant Secretary of State Winston Lord to withdraw U.S. support for a United Nations resolution criticizing China's human rights record. The resolution, entitled the "Situation of Human Rights in China," was a five-point document. Mr. Lord responded that the United States would continue to press forth with the resolution. The resolution, which was scheduled to come for a vote in the week that followed, was co-sponsored by the United States and the European Union. It was put before the United Nations Human Rights Commission in Geneva, whose delegates are drawn from 53 countries.[62]

On 8 March 1995—despite heavy European and U.S. support—China evaded criticism of its human rights record at the United Nations Human Rights Commission in Geneva. The resolution—which was defeated by a vote of 21 to 20—was opposed by Russia and Cuba. Brazil, Mexico, Venezuela and Egypt were among the twelve conferees that abstained. France approved the critical resolution. Assistant Secretary of State John Shattuck claimed that it was the first time that the commission had examined the human rights records of the Security Council members—and thus the China rights issue—at all.[63]

Two days later—on 10 March 1995—Foreign Minister Qian Qichen said that China would continue its human rights dialogue with the United States despite Washington's attempt to embarrass Beijing at the UN Human Rights Commission in Geneva.[64]

On 17 April 1995, the United States was unsuccessful in its attempt to persuade China to (1) end its nuclear cooperation with Iran; and (2) improve its human rights performance. The American initiative—which was posited by Secretary of State Christopher—materialized at a meeting of 174 nations at the United Nations in New York City to determine the future of the Nuclear Non-Proliferation Treaty.[65]

In the September 1994 issue of *Current History,* pro-democracy activist Chai Ling advocated a bilateral human rights commission comprising Chinese delegates from the National People's Congress and American delegates from Congress.[66] This worthy proposal, however, presupposes a high level of trust and confidence between the People's Republic and the United States.

The decision to improve the human-rights conditions in China can only come from the leadership of the Chinese Communist Party (CCP). It is likely that the CCP Politburo is seeking a dignified way to resolve this question.

That there is now a need for a positive, confidence-building initiative is beyond questions for Beijing's bilateral relations with Washington have evolved from cordial to confrontational.

China asserts that America's policy changed on 21 May 1995, when President Clinton decided to allow Taiwan President Lee Teng-hui to visit Cornell University (his alma mater).[67] Under the driving leadership of Sen. Frank H. Murkowski—the Republican from Alaska—the Congress voted overwhelmingly to allow a Taiwanese presidential visit. The Senate voted 97 to 1, and the House 396 to 0, in favor of a visa issuance.[68]

Since the Clinton Administration's decision to issue a visitor's visa to Lee Teng-hui, China has: (1) canceled talks on nuclear energy; (2) canceled negotiations on the control of ballistic missile technology; (3) postponed indefinitely the Defense Minister Chi Haotian's projected visit to the United States; (4) recalled an air force delegation; and (5) postponed a visit to Beijing by John Holum, the Director of the Arms Control and Disarmament Agency.[69]

A well-conceived overture to the Chinese leadership can reverse the current confrontational trend in Sino-American relations. There is reason to believe that such an initiative—with White House sponsorship—would win bipartisan support in Congress. Senator Max Baucus—the Montana Democrat—made the following observation on 19 April 1994:

We should always stand up for our values, but we need not assume that pressure and threats are the only way to get results. We should therefore develop "friendly" approaches that get results on human rights without threatening other priorities.[70]

In his Most-Favored-Nation speech of 26 May 1994, President Clinton clarified the need for a prestigious and dignified approach to the dilemma:

. . . every nation, every great nation makes some decisions and perhaps most decisions based on what is in the interest of the nation at that moment in time internally. But no nation

122

likes to feel that every decision it makes for the good, to do something that's right, that makes progress, is being made not because it's the right thing to do but only because of external pressure from someone else.[71]

President Clinton also used his address to broach an enduring question: "How can we best advance the cause of human rights and the other profound interests the United States has in our relationship with China?"[72]

Bilateral disputes often exist because each side has a legitimate case. It is only when a third factor or inducement is added to the equation that the prospect of flexibility and cooperation increases. The insertion of an inducement, especially if it is a positive and prestigious one, can create cooperation that had been theretofore nonexistent. It is the author's belief that the prospect of a Sino-American co-chairmanship of an international conference would suit the needs of policymakers in both Beijing and Washington. Put simply, an American overture of a conference co-chairmanship to resolve regional disputes is likely to compel Chinese leaders to favorably reconsider their repressive policies on human rights. Dr. Harry Harding of the George Washington University addressed this potentiality in his book, *A Fragile Relationship:*

A reversal of verdicts on the June 4 incident and progress toward political liberalization would reduce U.S. criticism of China's human rights record, and open more possibilities for academic and cultural exchange. With a renewed commitment to reform on the mainland, the prospects for the smooth return of Hong Kong to China and for some form of reconciliation between Taiwan and the mainland would be greatly enhanced. **A more pragmatic government in Peking would be more likely to find common ground with the United States on important regional and global secu-**

123

rity issues and more inclined to cooperate with the United States in addressing the emerging agenda of international economic, military, environmental, and social questions.[73] (Emphasis added)

On 3 July 1995—in a Beijing interview with reporters from Hungary and Germany—Pres. Jiang Zemin implored the United States to implement practical measures to restore the confidence that has dissipated since the decision to issue a U.S. visa to Taiwanese President Lee Teng-hui.[74] The international conference, which is outlined in the first section of this report, is designed to establish the prerequisite respect, trust, and confidence that are fundamental to an improvement in bilateral ties between the People's Republic of China and the United States of America.

Notes

1. Nicholas D. Kristof, "China Ousts Zhao and Picks Leaders Tough on Dissent," *New York Times,* 25 June 1989, p. 1; and Patrick E. Tyler, "Crossroads for China: With Democratic Stirrings among Chinese, U.S. Is Pressing Beijing on Crucial Choices," *New York Times,* 29 January 1994, p. 4.
2. "Wife Makes Plea for Jailed Chinese Official," *New York Times,* 15 May 1994, p. 20; and Sheryl WuDunn, "China Sentences an Ex-Official to 7 Years over Tiananmen Leaks," *New York Times,* 22 July 1992, p. A–3.
3. Philip Shenon, "Conversations/Zhu Muzhi: Want to Sell China's Record on Human Rights? Get Mr. Smooth," *New York Times,* 28 August 1994, p. IV–7.
4. "Jiang Gives Important Speech on Corruption," *FBIS-China,* 23 August 1993, pp. 18–20; Nicholas D. Kristof, "Beijing Promises Corruption Fight," *New York Times,* 22 August 1993, p. 7; and Patrick E. Tyler, "12 Intellectuals Petition China on Corruption," *New York Times,* 26 February 1995, p. 6.

124

5. Patrick E. Tyler, "China Detains and Then Frees a Top Dissident," *New York Times*, 5 March 1994, p. 4.

6. Ibid., p. 1; and "Shanghai Dissidents Held," *New York Times*, 9 April 1994, p. 4.

7. Steven Greenhouse, "China Is Releasing 2 Tibet Dissidents," *New York Times*, 15 January 1994, p. 5.

8. Seth Faison, "In Possible Signal, China Releases an Ailing Dissident," *New York Times*, 17 July 1995, p. A–4.

9. "Shanghai Dissidents Reportedly Jailed," *New York Times*, 12 October 1994, p. A–3.

10. U.S. Department of State Report: Human Rights in China, p. 16; and *China: Human Rights Violations Five Years after Tiananmen* (New York: Amnesty International, June 1994), p. 4.

11. U.S. Department of State Report: Human Rights in China, p. 16.

12. Philip Shenon, "Prison Sentences Seem Likely in Trial of 14 Chinese Dissidents," *New York Times*, 24 July 1994, p. 15.

13. Patrick E. Tyler, "As Deng Fades, China's Leaders Tighten Grip on Power," *New York Times*, 19 December 1994, p. A–3.

14. U.S. Department of State Report: Human Rights in China, p. 16; and Patrick E. Tyler, "Crossroads for China: With Democratic Stirrings among Chinese, U.S. Is Pressing Beijing on Crucial Choices," *New York Times*, 29 January 1994, p. 4.

15. *China: Human Rights Violations Five Years after Tiananmen* (New York: Amnesty International, June 1994), summary page and p. 30.

16. U.S. Department of State Report: Human Rights in China, p. 9; Amnesty International, op. cit., p. 31.

17. Amnesty International, op. cit., p. 30.

18. Ibid, p. 31.

19. U.S. Department of State Report: Human Rights in China, p. 10; and "4 Seized in Peking Pasting Up Posters," *New York Times*, 5 April 1979, p. A–14.

20. Patrick E. Tyler, "Eye on Olympics, China Frees Top Dissident," *New York Times*, 14 September 1993, p. A–6.

21. U.S. Department of State Report: Human Rights in China, p. 5; "Report to Congress Concerning Extension of Waiver Authority for the People's Republic of China," p. 6; Patrick E. Tyler, "China Arrests Leading Dissident For the Second Time in Month," *New York Times*, 2 April 994, p. 1.

22. Patrick E. Tyler, "Beijing Is Warning Leading Dissident," *New York*

Times, 27 February 1994, p. 4; and "Report to Congress Concerning Extension of Waiver Authority for the People's Republic of China," p. 6.

23. Amnesty International, op. cit., p. 4; Patrick E. Tyler, "China Says It Holds Dissident to Check 'New Crimes,' " *New York Times,* 5 April 1994, p. A–6; and Tyler, "Chinese Dissident Facing Possibility of New Charges," *New York Times,* 6 April 1994, p. A–12.

24. "Another Chinese Detained," *New York Times,* 7 April 1994, p. A–13.

25. Patrick E. Tyler, "China Arrests Leading Dissident for the Second Time in a Month," *New York Times,* 2 April 1994, p. 1; Patrick E. Tyler, "Beijing Is Warning Leading Dissident," *New York Times,* 27 February 1994, p. 4; Tyler, "Is Top Dissident Even Alive? Beijing Will Not Say," *New York Times,* 31 March 1995, p. A–10; U.S. Department of State Report: Human Rights in China, p. 9.

26. Patrick E. Tyler, "China Charges Leading Dissident with Trying to Overthrow Regime," *New York Times,* 22 November 1995, pp. A–1, A–7.

27. "Wife Makes Plea for Jailed Chinese Official," *New York Times,* 15 May 1994, p. 20.

28. Nicholas D. Kristof, "China Sentences 2 of Its Dissidents to 13-Year Terms," *New York Times,* 13 February 1991, p. A–1.

29. Patrick E. Tyler, "China Releases Dissident and Sends Him to U.S. for Treatment," *New York Times,* 24 April 1994, p. 6.

30. Patrick E. Tyler, "In a Surprise Gesture, China Releases a Major Dissident," *New York Times,* 14 May 1994, p. 7; Tyler, "As Deng Fades, China's Leaders Tighten Grip on Power," *New York Times,* 19 December 1994, p. A–3; "Chinese Dissident Reported Ill with Cancer," *New York Times,* 14 September 1994, p. A–3; U.S. Department of State Report: Human Rights in China, p. 4.

31. Patrick E. Tyler, "On Anniversary, Tiananmen Leader Speaks Out," *New York Times,* 5 June 1995, p. A–3; "Chinese Police Revoke Top Dissident's Parole," *New York Times,* 27 June, 1995, p. A–10; and Steven Mufson, "China Arrests, Raids Home of Dissident," *Washington Post,* 27 June 1995, p. A–14.

32. Patrick E. Tyler, "China's Discus Champ: Alone, Disabled and Barred," *New York Times,* 8 September 1994, p. A–3; and Tyler, "Chinese Hit by Tank Is Denied Place in Games," *New York Times,* 2 September 1994, p. A–5; Patrick E. Tyler, "China's First Family

Comes Under Growing Scrutiny," *New York Times,* 2 June 1995, p. A–3.

33. U.S. Department of State Report: Human Rights in China, pp. 8, 12; Patrick E. Tyler, "As Deng Fades, China's Leaders Tighten Grip on Power," *New York Times, 19 December 1994, p. A–3.*

34. Patrick E. Tyler, "China Dissident Reports Release," *New York Times,* 6 March 1994, p. 12.

35. Ibid., p. 12; U.S. Department of State Report: Human Rights in China, p. 5.

36. "Chinese Release Dissident After 6 Years in Prison," *New York Times,* 19 June 1995, p. A–2.

37. "China's Dissidents: Not As One," *The Economist,* 3 June 1995, p. 32; "Police in China Arrest Two More Dissidents," *New York Times,* 22 May 1995, p. A–4; and the U.S. Department of State Report: Human Rights in China, p. 10.

38. "Top China Dissident Is Reported Released," *New York Times,* 3 April 1994, p. 6; U.S. Department of State Report: Human Rights in China, p. 12.

39. Patrick E. Tyler, "Beijing Journal: A Dissident Finds the Political Prospects Bleak," *New York Times,* 16 April 1994, p. 4.

40. Patrick E. Tyler, "7 Chinese Intellectuals Appeal for End to Political Repression," *New York Times,* 11 March 1994, p. A–1; and Tyler, "12 Intellectuals Petition China On Corruption," *New York Times,* 26 February 1995, p. 6.

41. Steven Mufson, "China's Opposition on Defensive," *Washington Post,* 4 June 1995, p. A–27; and Patrick E. Tyler, "Crossroads for China: With Democratic Stirrings Among Chinese, U.S. is Pressing Beijing on Crucial Choices," *New York Times,* 29 January 1994, p. 1.

42. "Chinese Dissidents Issue Human Rights Demand," *Washington Post,* 28 February 1995, p. A–14.

43. Patrick E. Tyler, "12 Intellectuals Petition China on Corruption," *New York Times,* 26 February 1995, pp. 1, 6.

44. Patrick E. Tyler, "12 Chinese Intellectuals Call for Limit on Police Powers," *New York Times,* 3 March 1995, p. A–2.

45. "Chinese Dissidents Issue Human Rights Demand," *Washington Post,* 28 February 1995, p. A–14.

46. Patrick E. Tyler, "Scientists Urge Beijing to Stop Its Persecutions," *New York Times,* 16 May 1995, p. A–1.

127

47. "China's Congress to Ignore Dissidents' Calls," *New York Times,* 5 March 1995, p. 3.
48. U.S. Department of State Report; Human Rights in China, p. 19.
49. "Police in China Arrest Two More Dissidents," *New York Times,* 22 May 1995, p. A–5.
50. Ibid., p. 6; and *Universal Declaration of Human Rights,* United Nations Department of Public Information, DPI/876 (August 1993), pp. 8–10.
51. Ibid., pp. 13, 14, 19, 24; Amnesty International, op. cit., p. 4.
52. Patrick E. Tyler, "China Arrests Petitioner for Democracy," *New York Times,* 20 May 1995, p. 4.
53. "Chinese Police Broaden Crackdown on Dissidents," *New York Times,* 28 May 1995, p. 6; and Nicholas D. Kristof, "Hu Yaobang, 73, Dies in China; Led Communist Party in 1980's," *New York Times,* 15 April 1989, p. I–10.
54. Those products include wrenches, artificial flowers and diesel engines.
55. Steven Mufson, "China Claims American Recanted," *Washington Post,* 28 July 1995, pp. A–1, A–30.
56. Steven Mufson, "China Acknowledges Holding American," *Washington Post,* 28 June 1995, p. A–25; "China Detains Critic From U.S.," *Washington Post,* 27 June 1995, p. A–14; Elaine Sciolino, "In Warning to U.S., China Cracks Down on 2 Dissidents," *New York Times,* 29 June 1995, p. A–8; and "U.S. Protests Misdirection on Activist in China," *Washington Post,* 4 July 1995, p. A–17; "China Said to Detain Dissidents as Parley Nears," *New York Times,* 10 August 1995, p. A–3; and Keith B. Richburg, "U.S. Embassy Aide Visits American Jailed in China," *Washington Post,* 10 August 1995, p. A–23.
57. Warren Christopher, "U.S. National Interest in the Asia-Pacific Region," address to the National Press Club, Washington, D.C., 28 July 1995, p. 11.
58. James V. Feinerman, "Deteriorating Human Rights in China," *Current History,* Vol. 89, No. 548 (September 1990), p. 267.
59. Please refer to Patrick E. Tyler's articles: "U.S., Praising China, Is Still Wary on Rights," *New York Times,* 13 October 1993, p. A–15; and "China May Allow Red Cross to Visit Dissidents in Jail," *New York Times,* 10 November 1993, pp. A–1, A–17.
60. Patrick E. Tyler, "Abuses of Rights Persist in China Despite U.S.

Pleas," *New York Times,* 29 August 1994, p. A–1; and Tyler, "China Welcomes U.S. Trade Policy," *New York Times,* 28 May 1994, p. 5.

61. Patrick E. Tyler, "Abuses of Rights Persist in China Despite U.S. Pleas," *New York Times,* 29 August 1994, p. A–2; and "U.S. Can't Budge China on Human Rights," *Washington Times,* 16 January 1995, p. A–15.

62. Patrick E. Tyler, "U.S. and China in a Clash Over Human Rights," *New York Times,* 2 March 1995, p. A–7.

63. "U.N. Rights Panel Declines to Censure China," *New York Times,* 9 March 1995, p. A–5; and "Situation of Human Rights in China," text and voting record on resolution of the United Nations Commission on Human Rights, 7 and 8 March 1995, p. 6.

64. Patrick E. Tyler, "Chinese Aide Conciliatory Despite 'Foolish' U.S. Stand on Rights," *New York Times,* 11 March 1995, p. 5.

65. Elaine Sciolino, "Beijing Rebuffs U.S. on Halting Iran Atom Deal," *New York Times,* 18 April 1995, p. A–1.

66. "Tiananmen and China's Future: The View Five Years Later," *Current History,* Vol. 93, No. 584 (September 1994), pp. 247.

67. *New York Times* correspondent David W. Chen reported that during President Lee's visit, Senators D'Amato (New York), Helms (North Carolina) and Murkowski (Alaska) visited the Cornell campus. U.S. Congressman Gary Ackerman (New York) also visited the Taiwanese President. David W. Chen, "Taiwan's President Tiptoes Around Politics at Cornell," *New York Times,* 10 June 1995, p. 4.

68. Steven Greenhouse, "Officials Say Clinton Will Defy Beijing on Taiwan Visa," *New York Times,* 22 May 1995, p. A–6; and Daniel Southerland, "First Private Visit to U.S. Completed, Taiwan President Mulls Trip to Alaska," *Washington Post,* 11 June 1995, p. A–26.

69. Elaine Sciolino, "Angered Over Taiwan, China Summons Home Its Ambassador," *New York Times,* 17 June 1995, p. 5.

70. Senator Maxwell Baucus, "A Strategy For Human Rights in China: White Paper," 19 April 1994, p. 10.

71. William J. Clinton, "The President's News Conference of 26 May 1994," *Weekly Compilation of Presidential Documents,* Vol. 30, No. 21 (30 May 1994), p. 1168.

72. Ibid., p. 1166.

73. Harry Harding, op. cit., pp. 309–310.

74. Mark O'Neil, "China Urges U.S. Action to Repair Ties," *Washington Post,* 4 July 1995, p. A–17.

129

References

Primary Sources

"Arafat's Beijing Speech," *FBIS-China*, 10 October 1989, pp. 12–13.
"Article Discusses Possibilities for Clinton Visit," *FBIS-China*, 6 September 1994, pp. 4, 5.
"Article Salutes U.S. Secretary Brown's Visit," *FBIS-China*, 7 September 1994, pp. 1, 2.
Baucus, Sen. Maxwell. "American China Policy in 1994: Trade, Human Rights and Our Future in Asia," American Enterprise Institute, Washington, D.C., 10 May 1994, 7 pp.
————. "A Strategy for Human Rights in China," 25 March 1994, 5 pp.
————. "China Policy in the Age of Pacific Community," Remarks of Sen. Max Baucus to the U.S. China Business Council, 19 January 1995, 8 pp.
————. "Floor Statement on MFN Conditions," 20 May 1993, 3 pp.
————. "Floor Statement on China Human Rights Policy," 16 March 1994, 3 pp.
————. "Opening Remarks on Debate on MFN Conditions for China," National Press Club Newsmaker Luncheon, 19 April 1994, 4 pp.
————. "Sources and Prospects for American China Policy," Hong Kong American Chamber of Commerce, 26 August 1993, 6 pp.
————. "A Strategy for Human Rights in China: White Paper," 19 April 1994, 12 pp.
————. "Where We Stand and Where We Go from Here: China Policy in 1994 and Beyond," Remarks of Sen. Max Baucus to the U.S.–China Business Council, 27 January 1994, 8 pp.

131

"Beijing, U.S. Sign Accord on Flood Forecast Capabilities," *FBIS-China*, 30 August 1994, pp. 6, 7.

"Bentsen Cochairs Joint Economic Committee Meeting," *FBIS-China*, 21 January 1994, pp. 4–6.

Berger, Samuel R. "Most-Favored-Nation for China," *Good Morning America*, 27 May 1994 (Show #2075), p. 2.

Bradley, Sen. Bill, "Floor Statement by Senator Bill Bradley on China's Most Favored Nation Status," 18 May 1994, 5 pp.

Brittan, Sir Leon. "A Long Term Policy for China-Europe Relations," European Commission Document COM (95)279/3, O/95/215, Brussels, 29 June 1995.

"Brown's Delegation Arrives in Guangzhou," *FBIS-China*, 9 September 1994, p. 75.

China: Human Rights Violations Five Years after Tiananmen (New York: Amnesty International, June 1994), 48 pp.

Christopher, Warren. "U.S. National Interest in the Asia-Pacific Region," Address by the Secretary of State to the National Press Club, Washington, D.C., 28 July 1995, 17 pp.

Clinton, William J., "Remarks to the Nixon Center for Peace and Freedom Policy Conference: 1 March 1995," *Weekly Compilation of Presidential Documents*, Vol. 31, No. 9 (6 March 1995), pp. 339–44.

———. "Report to Congress Concerning Extension of Waiver Authority for the People's Republic of China," 28 May 1993, *Public Papers of the Presidents of the United States: William J. Clinton, Book One* (Washington: U.S. Government Printing Office, 1993), pp. 772–76.

———. "Statement on Most-Favored-Nation Trade Status for China: 28 May 1993," *Public Papers of the Presidents of the United States: William J. Clinton, Book One* (Washington: U.S. Government Printing Office, 1994), pp. 770, 771.

———. "The President's News Conference of 26 May 1994," *Weekly Compilation of Presidential Documents*, Vol. 30, No. 21 (30 May 1994), pp. 1,166–1,171.

"Commentary Views Significance of Ron Brown's Visit," *FBIS-China*, 6 September 1994, pp. 3, 4.

"Coverage on Jiang Zemin's 'Reunification' Speech," *FBIS-China,* 30 January 1995, pp. 84–90.

"Executive Order: Conditions for Renewal of Most Favored Nation Status for the People's Republic of China in 1994," The White House, Office of the Press Secretary, 28 May 1993, 2 pp.

"Foreign Ministry Holds Weekly News Conference: Spokesman Comments on Perry Visit," *FBIS-China,* 20 October 1994, p. 1.

"Full Text of PRC-French Communiqué," *FBIS-China,* 6 October 1989, pp. 10–12.

Hamilton, Congressman Lee H. "The United States and China: Toward a Policy of Realism," Remarks by Congressman Hamilton to the American Enterprise Institute, 10 May 1994, 5 pp.

"Israel's Rabin Holds Talks with Qian Qichen," *FBIS-China,* 18 September 1992, p. 13.

"Jiang Gives Important Speech on Corruption," *FBIS-China,* 23 August 1993, pp. 18–20.

"Jiang Urges Relations with U.S. Based on Equality," *FBIS-China,* 18 January 1995, pp. 4, 5.

"Jiang Zemin, Brown Meet, Discuss Relations," *FBIS-China,* 30 August 1994, pp. 3, 5.

"Jiang Zemin Meets Perry, Calls for Cooperation," *FBIS-China,* 20 October, pp. 5–7.

Li Daoyu. "Foreign Policy and Arms Control: The View from China," *Arms Control Today,* Vol. 23, No. 10 (December 1993), pp. 9–11.

Li Teng-hui, "Always in My Heart; An Olin Lecture," delivered at Cornell University, Ithaca, New York, 9 June 1995, 12 pp.

"Li Peng, Brown Meet, Discuss Bilateral Relations," *FBIS-China,* 30 August 1994, pp. 2, 3.

"Li Peng Hopes Perry Visit to Play 'Positive Role,' " *FBIS-China,* 15 March 1994, p. 9.

"Liu Huaqing, Perry Hold 'Friendly' Talks ," *FBIS-China,* 18 October 1994, pp. 4–6.

Lord, Winston, Assistant Secretary for East Asian and Pacific Affairs. "Mid-Term Review of Most-Favored-Nation Status for China: Statement before the Subcommittee on Trade of the House Ways and Means Committee, Washington, D.C., February 24, 1994," *U.S. Department of State Dispatch,* Vol. 5, No. 10, (7 March 1994): pp. 127–130.

"Media Commentary on Commerce Secretary Brown's Visit," *FBIS-China,* 1 September 1994, pp. 5, 6.

"Qian Qichen Addresses UN General Assembly," *FBIS-China,* 26 September 1991, pp. 2–8.

"Qian Qichen Arrives in Israel; Met by Peres," *FBIS-China,* 16 September 1992, pp. 11, 13.

"Qian Qichen Concludes Visit to Israel on 18 September," *FBIS-China,* 22 September 1992, pp. 13, 14.

"Qian Qichen Discusses Sino–U.S. Relations," *FBIS-China,* 15 March 1994, pp. 6–8.

"Qian Qichen in Israel, Reiterates F-16 Position," *FBIS-China,* 17 September 1992, p. 14.

"Qian Qichen Interviewed on African Situation, Policy," *FBIS-China,* 24 January 1994, pp. 14, 15.

"Qian Qichen 'Somewhat Disappointed' with U.S. Secretary's Visit," *FBIS-China,* 16 May 1994, pp. 5, 6.

"Qian Returns from Trip," *FBIS-China,* 25 January 1994, pp. 9, 10.

"Qian, U.S. Counterpart Warren Christopher Meet," *FBIS-China,* 25 January 1994, pp. 7–9.

"Reportage on Energy Secretary O'Leary's Trip," *FBIS-China,* 21 February 1995, pp. 2–5.

Resolutions and Decisions of the Security Council: 1990, United Nations Document S/INF/46 (United Nations, New York, 1991), 34 pp.

Resolutions and Decisions of the Security Council, 1991, United Nations Document S/INF/47 (New York: United Nations, 1991), 65 pp.

"Shanghai, U.S. Sign Electric Agreement," *FBIS-China,* 2 September 1994, pp. 33, 34.

"Situation of Human Rights in China," Text and Voting Record on Resolution of the United Nations Commission on Human Rights, 7 and 8 March 1995, 6 pp.

"Statement by H. E. Qian Qichen, Vice-Premier and Minister of Foreign Affairs, and Chairman of the Delegation of the People's

Republic of China at Forty-ninth session of the United Nations General Assembly, 28 September 1994," 9 pp.

"Secretary Brown's Mission to China Leads to Breakthroughs in Trade," *Business America* (October 1994): pp. 29–31.

Shattuck, John. "Human Rights and Democracy in Asia: Address to the Asia Foundations' Center for Asian Pacific Affairs, Alexandria, Virginia, June 28, 1994," *U.S. Department of State Dispatch,* Vol. 5, No. 29, 18 July 19944, pp. 480–84.

Spero, Joan E., Under Secretary for Economic and Agricultural Affairs. "The International Economic Agenda and the State Department's Role: Excerpts from Address before the Congressional International Economic Issues Forum, Washington, D.C., February 25, 1994," *U.S. Department of State Dispatch,* Vol. 5, No. 10 (March 1994): pp. 123–25.

"Text of President Lee Teng-hui's Unification Speech," *FBIS-China,* 10 April 1995, pp. 77–80.

"United Nations General Assembly Resolution 36/120C: Question of Palestine, 10 December 1981," *Resolutions and Decisions Adopted by the General Assembly during its Thirty-sixth Session.* (New York: United Nations, 1982), p. 27.

Universal Declaration of Human Rights, United Nations Department of Public Information, DPI/876 (August 1993), 16 pp.

"U.S. Boeing Company Supports MFN Status," *FBIS-China,* 16 May 1994, p. 6.

"U.S. Commerce Secretary Brown Tours Shanghai," *FBIS-China,* 1 September 1994, p. 5.

"U.S. Commerce Secretary's Remarks Cited," *FBIS-China,* 7 September 1994, p. 1.

"U.S. Defense Secretary Perry Arrives in Beijing," *FBIS-China,* 17 October 1994, pp. 11–13

"U.S. Secretary of Defense Weinberger Visits China," *FBIS-China,* 10 October 1986, pp. B1–B5.

"U.S. Secretary of State Meets PRC Leaders," *FBIS-China,* 14 March 1994, pp. 3–9.

"U.S. Treasury Secretary Bentsen on Official Visit," *FBIS-China,* 19 January 1994, pp. 2, 3.

"U.S. Treasury Secretary Bentsen Continues Visit," *FBIS-China,* 21 January 1994, pp 2–6.

"Wu, Brown Sign Landmark Accord to Expand Commercial Ties," *FBIS-China,* 30 August 1994, pp. 5, 6.

"XINHUA Cites Secretary Brown on Bilateral Trade Ties," *FBIS-China,* 6 September 1994, p. 3.

"XINHUA Quotes Brown in Hong Kong on MFN Status," *FBIS-China,* 7 September 1994, p. 1.

"XINHUA Reports on Brown's News Conference," *FBIS-China,* 31 August 1994, pp. 1–4.

Secondary Sources

"Another Chinese Detained," *New York Times,* 7 April 1994, p. A–13.

"Appeal for China Dissident," *New York Times. 28 September 1994, p. A–6.*

Apple, R.W., Jr. "A Quarrel Obscured: Squabble over Site of Private Talks Cloaks Dispute on Recognizing Israel," *New York Times,* 2 November 1991, p. 4.

Apple, R.W., Jr. "Syrians Balking but Other Arabs Favor More Talks: An Impasse over the Site; Israel Wants Mideast Location While Its Opponents Seek to Continue in Madrid," *New York Times,* 3 November 1991, pp. 1, 22.

Archibald, George. "GOP Leaders Urge Withdrawal from U.N. Women's Conference," *The Washington Times,* 14 July 1995, p. A–10.

Ashrawi, Hanan. *This Side of Peace: A Personal Account* (New York: Simon & Schuster, 1995), 318 pp.

"At Home, Taiwan Leader Hints at Visit to Japan," *New York Times,* 13 June 1995, p. A–12.

Barber, Ben, and George Archibald. "White House, Congress Clash on China Policy," *The Washington Times,* 14 July 1995, pp. A–1, A–10.

"Beijing Praises Decision," *New York Times,* 27 May 1994, p. A–8.

"Bentsen Says China Would Lose Trade Status Now," *New York Times,* 19 March 1994, p. 3.

Bonner, Raymond. "Balkan Conflict's Spread to Macedonia Is Feared," *New York Times,* 9 April 1995, p. 12.

Bradley, Bill. "Trade, the Real Engine of Democracy," *New York Times,* 25 May 1994, p. A–21.

Bradsher, Keith. "Bill to Restrict China's Imports Loses in House," *New York Times,* 10 August 1994, p. A–7.

———. "House Votes Curbs on Chinese Imports," *New York Times,* 11 July 1991, p. A–3.

———. "Senate Restricts Trade with Cina; Bush Veto Likely," *New York Times,* 24 July 1991, pp. A–1, A–9.

Brauchli, Marcus W. "Imposition of Trade Sanctions Exposes a Contradictory U.S. Approach to China," *Wall Street Journal,* 7 February 1995, p. A–19.

Calabrese, John. *China's Changing Relations with the Middle East* (London and New York: Pinter Publishers, 1991), 183 p.

Chang, Leslie, and Kathy Chen. "China's Planned Guided-Missile Tests Seem Aimed at Intimidating Taiwan," *The Wall Street Journal,* 20 July 1995, p. A–8.

Chen, David W. "Taiwan's President Tiptoes around Politics at Cornell," *New York Times,* 10 June 1995, p. 4.

Chen, Kathy. "U.S. Business Interests in China Lash Out at Washington for Hurting Bottom Line," *The Wall Street Journal,* 6 July 1995, p. A–5.

———. "Sino–U.S. Relations Back to Square One," *The Wall Street Journal,* 1 September 1995, p. A–4.

———. "U.S.–China Relations Strained Further by Charges of Espionage against Wu," *The Wall Street Journal,* 10 July 1995, p. A–10.

"China: A Jewish Question," *The Economist* (3 December 1994): p. 46.

"China and Taiwan to Extend talks in Singapore by a Day," *New York Times,* 29 April 1993, p. A–3.

"China Asks Clinton to Reaffirm Policy on Taiwan's Status," *New York Times,* 13 July 1995, p. 1.

"China Detains Critic from U.S.," *Washington Post,* 27 June 1995, p. A–14.

"China Lambastes U.S. Bill," Washington Post, 23 July 1995, p. A–17.

"China Makes Trade Pleas," *New York Times,* 12 September 1994, p. D–4.

"China Releases 3 Prisoners in Gesture to U.S.," *New York Times,* 5 February 1994, p. 4.

"China Revokes Passport of Expelled Labor Leader," *New York Times,* 22 August 1993, p. 6.

"China Said to Detain Dissidents as Parley Nears," *New York Times,* 10 August 1995, p. A–3.

"China's Bad Report Card," *New York Times,* 9 February 1994, p. A–20.

"China's Congress to Ignore Dissidents' Calls," *New York Times,* 5 March 1995, p. 3.

"China's Dissidents: Not as one," *The Economist* (3 June 1995): p. 32, 33.

"China Sending Its Ambassador Back to U.S. as Feud Subsides," *New York Times,* 29 August 1995, p. A–8.

"China Sends Home Ailing Dissident," *Washington Post,* 16 July 1995, p. A–24.

"China Tests Nuclear Bomb," *New York Times,* 16 May 1995, p. A–8.

"China Warns It Will Retaliate If U.S. Proceeds with Sanctions," *New York Times,* 1 January 1995, p. 14.

"China Warns U.S. over Taiwan Visitor," *New York Times,* 26 May 1995, p. A–5.

"Chinese Cancel Talks on Weapons Questions," *New York Times,* 29 May 1995, p. 2.

"Chinese Dissident Reported Ill with Cancer," *New York Times,* 14 September 1994, p. A–3.

"Chinese Dissidents Issue Human Rights Demand," *Washington Post,* 28 February 1995, p. A–14.

"Chinese Police Broaden Crackdown on Dissidents," *New York Times,* 28 May 1995, p. 6.

"Chinese Police Revoke Top Dissident's Parole," *New York Times,* 27 June 1995, p. A–10.

"Chinese Release Dissident after 6 Years in Prison," *New York Times,* 19 June 1995, p. A–2.

"Chinese Repression: Still an Issue," *New York Times,* 28 July 1994, p. 22.

"Christopher Argues against Snubbing China," *Washington Post,* 17 July 1995, p. A–20.

"Climbing a Tree to Catch a Fish," *New York Times,* 11 March 1994, p. A–10.

"Clinton Renews Trade Privileges for China Despite Rights Record," *New York Times,* 3 June 1995, p. 3.

"Communications Satellites; The Long March Back to China," *The Economist* (5 November 1994): pp. 67, 68.

Cohen, Roger. "As Truce Dies, Bosnia Rejects Extension," *New York Times,* 1 May 1995, p. A–10.

———. "Conflict in the Balkans; Peackeeping vs. Intractable War," *New York Times,* 11 June 1995, p. 14.

———. "U.N. Chief Orders Review of Peacekeeping Mission in Bosnia," *New York Times,* 13 May 1995, p. 3.

Constantine, Gus. "Chinese Dissident's Friend Decried Arrest," *Washington Times,* 6 July 1995, pp. A–1, A–10.

Cooper, Helene, and Robert S. Greenberger. "U.S. and China Agree to Meet Next Week in Fresh Attempt to Avert a Trade War," *Wall Street Journal,* 7 February 1995, pp. A–2, A–12.

Coswell, Alan. "Israel and Arabs, Face to Face, Begin Quest for Mideast Peace: In Contact at Last, but Never Eye to Eye," *New York Times,* 31 October 1991, pp. A–1, A–18.

———. "Seeking China Deal, Bonn Shuns Rights Issue," *New York Times,* 13 July 1995, p. A–8.

Crossette, Barbara. "China Breaks Ranks with Other Nuclear Nations on Treaty," *New York Times,* 19 April 1995, p. A–16.

———. "China Signs Agreement with U.S. to Cut Exports Made by Prisoners," *New York Times,* 8 August 1992, p. 3.

———. "Chinese Won't Yield on Isolating a Global Women's Forum," *New York Times,* 25 May 1995, p. A–12.

———. "Consensus Seen for Indefinite Extension of Nuclear Pact," *New York Times,* 7 May 1995, p. 21.

————. "Many Empty Seats at Mideast Talks," *New York Times*, 12 May, 1992, p. A–6.

————. "New Role Sought for U.N. Bosnia Force," *New York Times*, 17 May 1995, p. A–6.

Davis, Bob. "House Drops Threat of Trade Sanctions against China after Voting for Censure," *The Wall Street Journal*, 21 July 1995, p. A–2.

————. "U.S. Likely to Keep China's MFN Status," *The Wall Street Journal*, 18 July 1995, pp. A–2, A–11.

"Defending Taiwan," *The Economist* (12 November 1994): pp. 41, 42.

Dobbs, Michael. "Christopher Treads Lightly on China Policy," *Washington Post*, 1 August 1995, p. A–15.

————. "U.S., China Agree to talks on Relations," *Washington Post*, 2 August 1995, p. A–27, A–29.

"Egypt and Israel End Their Political Chilliness," *New York Times*, 10 June 1995, p. 4.

"EU Calls for U.S., China to Soften Dispute on WTO," *The Wall Street Journal*, 6 July 1995, p. A–5.

"Excerpts from Petition against Chinese Corruption," *New York Times*, 26 February 1995, p. 6.

"Excerpts from Petition to China's Leaders," *New York Times*, 16 May 1995, p. A–12.

"Excerpts from Statement on Zhao's Dismissal," *New York Times*, 25 June 1989, p. 12.

Faison, Seth. "A Business Deal Makes a Point for China," *New York Times*, 16 July 1995, p. 6.

————. "China Accuses Two U.S. Officers of Spying and Will Expel Them," *New York Times*, 3 August 1995, pp. A–1, A–11.

————. "China Closes a Disk Factory as Sanctions Deadline Nears," *New York Times*, 26 February 1995, p. 6.

————. "China Says Detained American Rights Advocate Admits Falsifying TV Documentaries," *New York Times*, 28 July 1995, p. A–6.

————. "Fighting Piracy and Frustration in China," *New York Times*, 17 May 1995, pp. D–1, D–5.

———. "In Possible Signal, China Releases an Ailing Dissident," *New York Times,* 17 July 1995, p. A–4.

———. "Politics Aside, Many in China Are Expanding Business with Taiwan," *New York Times,* 11 July 1995, p. A–8.

———. "Taiwan Reports Nearby Firing of 4 Test Missiles by China," *New York Times,* 24 July 1995, p. A–2.

———. "U.S. and China Sign Accord to End Piracy of Software, Music Recordings and Film," *New York Times,* 27 February 1995, pp. A–1, D–6.

Feinerman, James V. "Deteriorating Human Rights in China," *Current History,* Vol. 89, No. 548 (September 1990), pp. 265–269, 279, 280.

———. "Human Rights in China," *Current History,* Vol. 88, No. 539 (September 1989), pp. 273–276, 293–295.

Fewsmith, Joseph. "America and China: Back from the Brink," *Current History,* Vol. 93, No. 584 (September 1994), pp. 250–55.

"French Leader's Trip to China Criticized," *New York Times,* 12 April 1994, p. A–11.

Friedman, Thomas L. "A Missing Olive Branch," *New York Times,* 20 October 1991, pp. 1, 10.

———. "Arab-Israel Talks on Regional Issues Start in Moscow," *New York Times,* 29 January 1992, pp. A–1, A–8.

———. "Bentsen Says China Isn't Doing Enough on Rights," *New York Times,* 20 January 1994, p. A–6.

———. "China May Allow U.S. Broadcasts," *New York Times,* 18 May 1994, pp. A–1, A–8.

———. "China Warns U.S. on Taiwan Jet Deal," *New York Times,* 4 September 1992, p. A–3.

———. "Deal with China Urged by Bentsen," *New York Times,* 20 March 1994, p. 20.

———. "Democrats Press for a Compromise on Chinese Trade," *New York Times,* 21 April 1994, pp. A–1, A–6.

———. "In First Direct Negotiation, Israelis and Palestinians Agree to Discuss Self-Rule: A Step Ahead in Madrid," *New York Times,* 4 November 1991, pp. A–1, A–8.

———. "Israel and Arabs, Face to Face, Begin Quest for Mideast

141

Peace; First Full Meeting," *New York Times,* 31 October 1991, pp. A–1, A–16.

―――. "Legislator Urges Diplomacy to Improve Rights in China," *New York Times,* 11 May 1994, p. A–12.

―――. "Mideast Session Adjourns, with Prospects Uncertain for Second Phase of Talks," *New York Times,* 2 November 1991, pp. 1, 4.

―――. "No Smooth Talk: Amid Histrionics, Arabs and Israelis Team Up to Lose an Opportunity," *New York Times,* 3 November 1991, pp. IV–1, 4.

―――. "Senator Asks End to Threats against China," *New York Times,* 27 January 1994, p. A–11.

―――. "U.S. and China Widen Accords on Civil Rights," *New York Times,* 21 January 1994, pp. A–1, A–9.

―――. "U.S. Is to Maintain Trade Privileges for China's Goods; Clinton Votes for Business," *New York Times,* 27 May 1994, pp. A–1, –8.

―――. "U.S. May Ease Rights Goals with Beijing," *New York Times,* 24 March 1994, pp. A–1, A–13.

―――. "U.S. Now Expects the Mideast Talks to Take Time Out," *New York Times,* 5 November 1991, pp. A–1, A–12.

―――. "U.S. Shift on Beijing: Will Embrace Win Change?" *New York Times,* 23 January 1994, p. 10.

―――. "Waiters at the Table: Soviets Serve U.S. Needs for Parley in Hopes of Winning Economic Help," *New York Times,* 30 October 1991, p. A–11.

Gargan, Edward A. "Gauging the Consequences of Spurning China," *New York Times,* 21 March 1994, pp. D–1, D–5.

―――. "In China, Art of the Raw Deal," *New York Times,* 12 February 1995, p. IV–5.

―――. "Taiwan Enthralled by President's 'Private' U.S. Trip," *New York Times,* 8 June 1995, p. A–3.

Giacomo, Carol. "U.S. Urges China to Reconsider Boycott of Arms Talks," *Reuters, Ltd.,* 16 September 1992, p. 2.

Godwin, Paul H. B. And John J. Schulz, "China and Arms Control: Transition in East Asia," *Arms Control Today,* Vol. 24, No. 9 (November 1994): pp. 8–111.

Godman, David S., and Gerald Segal, editors. *China in the Nineties: Crisis Management and Beyond* (Oxford: Clarendon Press, 1992), 226 pp.

Gordon, Michael R. "Perry Visit Seeks to Rebuild Ties with Chinese Military," *New York Times*, 17 October 1994, p. A–8.

———. "U.S. to China: Be More Open on Arms Plan," *New York Times*, 19 October 1994, p. A–14.

Greenberg, Joel. "Israel and P.L.O. to Miss Target Date for New Accord," *New York Times*, 19 June 1995, p. A–2.

Greenberger, Robert S. "Clinton Expected to Assure China abut Relations," *The Wall Street Journal*, 31 July 1995, p. A–10.

———. "U.S. and China Agree to Resume Talks after a Rocky Two Months of Feuding." *The Wall Street Journal*, 2 August 1995, p. A–4.

———. "U.S. and China: A Trail of Misperceptions," *The Wall Street Journal*, 14 July 1995, p. A–8.

———. "Relations Worsen between U.S., China as Suspicions, Anger Foment Disputes," *The Wall Street Journal*, 5 July 1995, p. A–10.

Greenhouse, Steven, "Aide Says U.S. May Scrap an Across-the-Board Penalty for China," *New York Times*, 30 March 1994, p. A–10.

———. "China Arrests Start a Dispute in Washington," *New York Times*, 4 August 1995, pp. A–1 A–4.

———. "China is Releasing 2 Tibet Dissidents," *New York Times*, 15 January 1994, p. 5.

———. "Christopher Feels Capitol Hill Heat on China," *New York Times*, 25 May 1994, p. A–5.

———. "Christopher Presses Policy of Engagement with Asia," *New York Times*, 28 May 1994, p. 5.

———. "Clinton Meets with Bosnian and Croation Chiefs," *New York Times*, 17 March 1995, p. A–9.

———. "Officials Say Clinton Will Defy Beijing on Taiwan Visa," *New York Times*, 22 May 1995, p. A–6.

———. "President Condemns Beijing; Christopher Visit Questioned," *New York Times*, 5 March 1994, p. 4.

———. "State Dept. Castigates China on Rights Record," *New York Times,* 2 February 1994. p. A–9.

———. "U.S. and Russia Agree to Try to Extend Fraying Bosnia Cease-Fire," *New York Times,* 24 March 1995, p. A–5.

———. "Years Effort by 5-Nation Group Accomplishes Little in Sosnia," *New York Times,* 22 March 1995, p. A–8.

———. "$1 Billion in Sales of High-Tech Items to China Blocked," *New York Times,* 26 August 1993, pp. A–1, A–15.

Grier, Peter. "Why a Bamboo Curtain Has Fallen on Relations between U.S. and China," *The Christian Science Monitor* (7 July 1995): pp. 1, 9.

Haberman, Clyde. "In a Cold Setting, Numbing Speeches," *New York Times,* 29 January 1992, p. A–8.

———. "Mideast Parley Ends in Moscow under Shadow: Palestinians Role Hazy as New Talks Are Set," *New York Times,* 30 January 1992, pp. A–1, A–10.

Hamilton, Martha M., and Steven Mufson, "Clinton Hails Accord with China on Trade," *Washington Post,* 27 February 1995, pp. A–1, A–16.

Harding, Harry. *A Fragile Relationship: The United States and China since 1972* (Washington, D.C.: The Brookings Institution, 1992), 458 pp.

Harris, Lillian Craig. *China Considers the Middle East* (New York: I. B. Tauris & Co., Ltd., 1993), 345 pp.

House, Karen Elliot. "Drifting toward Disaster in Asia," *The Wall Street Journal,* 26 July 1995, p. A–12.

"How to Lose the Olympics," *New York Times,* 9 September 1994, p. A–26.

Ibrahim, Youssef M. "In First Direct Negotiation, Israelis and Palestinians Agree to Discuss Self-Rule: Baker is Optimistic," *New York Times,* 4 November 1991, pp. A–1, A–8.

———. "Syria's Tough Choice: Changes in Relationship in Mideast Shift Balance of Power in the Region," *New York Times,* 3 November 1991, p. 22.

"Iraq Says China Vows to Work Against Sanctions," *Washington Times,* 4 July 1995, p. A–8.

144

Jehl, Douglas. "Clinton Makes No Progress with Beijing," *New York Times,* 3 May 1994, p. A–8.

———. "Clinton Stresses China Rights Goal," *New York Times,* 25 March 1994, p. A–12.

———. "U.S. Is to Maintain Trade Privileges for China's Goods: A Policy Reversal," *New York Times,* 27 May 1994, pp. A–1, A–8.

Johnston, David Cay. "Cautious Praise for Pact from U.S. Business," *New York Times,* 27 February 1995, pp. D–1, D–6.

Kahn, Joseph. "China Expels 2 U.S. Officers on Spy Charge," *Wall Street Journal,* 3 August 1995, p. A–6.

———. "Motorola Gets Criticism in Shanghai for Its Cellular Telephone Network," *The Wall Street Journal,* 14 July 1995, p. A–8.

Kovaleski, Serge F. "Gingrich Backs Ties with Taiwan," *The Washington Post,* 10 July 1995, pp. A–1, A–12.

Kristof, Nicholas D. "After Four Decades of Bitterness, China and Taiwan Plan to Meet," *New York Times,* 12 April 1993, pp. A–1, A–5.

———. "Beijing Promises Corruption Fight," *New York Times,* 22 August 1993, p. 7.

———. "China and Taiwan Have First Talks," *New York Times,* 28 April 1993, p. A–8.

———. "China Ousts Zhao and Picks Leaders Tough on Dissent," *New York Times,* 25 June 1989, pp. 1, 12.

———. "China Says U.S. Is Harassing Ship Suspected of Taking Arms to Iran," *New York Times,* 9 August 1993, p. A–6.

———. "China Sentences 2 of Its Dissidents to 13-Year Terms," *New York Times,* 13 February 1991, pp. A–1, A–11.

———. "China Sentences 8 Leading Dissidents," *New York Times,* 27 January 1991, p. 3.

———. "Hu Yaobang, 73, Dies in China; Led Communist Party in 1980's," *New York Times,* 15 April 1989, p. I–10.

———. "Starting to Build Their First Bridge, China and Taiwan Sign 4 Pacts," *New York Times,* 30 April 1993, p. A–11.

———. "The World: More Than One Way to Squeeze China," *New York Times,* 22 May 1994, p. IV–5.

Laris, Michael. "China Convicts American of Spying," *Washington Post,* 24 August 1995, pp. A–1, A–29.

Lewis, Anthony. "Abroad at Home: A Chinese Puzzle," *New York Times,* 12 June 1995, p. A–15.

Lim, Benjamin Kang. "Rights, Taiwan Issues Stress U.S.–China Relations," *The Washington Times,* 12 July 1995, p. A–17.

Lippman, Thomas W. "Envoys Offer Evidence of Waning U.S. Muscle," *Washington Post,* 28 May 1995, p. A–37.

———. "U.S. Sees Engagement in Current Policy, but China Feels Containment," *Washington Post,* 9 July 1995, p. A–23.

Liu, Binyan, "Tiananmen and the Future of China," *Current History* Vol. 93, No. 584 (September 1994), pp. 241–46.

"Looking Casual, Japan's Prime Minister Ends Visit to China," *New York Times,* 22 March 1994, p. A–6.

Manegold, Catherine S. "A.F.L.-C.I.O. Leader Urges End to China's Current Trade Status," *New York Times,* 14 April 1994, p. A–6.

———. "Senate Told of China Convicts Shot for Organs," *New York Times,* 5 May 1995, p. A–10.

———. "German-Chinese Deals Ringing Hollow," *The Wall Street Journal,* 14 July 1995, p. A–8.

———. "Germany Awaits China-Policy Payoff," *The Wall Street Journal,* 11 July 1995, p. A–10.

Mead, Walter Russell. "The Danger of Bigger Trouble with the Chinese," *New York Times,* 15 August 1995, p. A–17.

Montagnon, Peter and Laura Tyson. "Taiwan Takes Long Shot at World Recognition," *Financial Times,* 25 July 1995, p. 5.

———. "American Charged in China," *Washington Post,* 9 July 1995, pp. A–1, A–23.

Mufson, Steven. "American Visited in China," *Washington Post,* 11 July 1995, p. A–12.

———. "China Acknowledges Holding American," *Washington Post,* 28 June 1995, p. A–14.

———. "China Arrests, Raids Home of Dissident," *Washington Post,* 27 June 1995, p. A–14.

———. "China Claims American Recanted," *Washington Post,* 28 July 1995, pp. A–1, A–30.

————. "China's Corruption 'Virus,' " *Washington Post,* 22 July 1995, p. A–16.

————. "China Lists Charges against Detainees," *Washington Post,* 4 May 1995, p. A–34.

————. "China Says Crackdown on CD Pirates Widens," *Washington Post,* 16 February 1995, p. A–34.

————. "China Recalls Ambassador to U.S. to Protest Visa to Taiwan Leader," *Washington Post,* 17 June 1995, p. A–14.

————. "China's Opposition on Defensive," *Washington Post,* 4 June 1995, pp. A–1, A–26, A–27.

————. "China to Conduct Military Exercise Near Taiwan," *Washington Post,* 19 July 1995, p. A–18.

————. "China Views Lee's U.S. Visit as Affront," *Washington Post,* 8 June 1995, p. A–18.

————. "China Movement Seeks Rule of Law to Keep Government in Check," *Washington Post,* 5 March 1995, pp. A–25, A–31.

————. "Red Chinese Tape: Beijing Bureaucracy Seen Impeding Women's Conclave," *Washington Post,* 28 July 1995, pp. A–29, A–30.

————. "Sino-U.S. Relations 'Pushed Into a Danger Zone,' " *Washington Post,* 21 June 1995, p. A–17.

————. "U.S., China Sign Trade Act but Bicker Over an Earlier Accord," *Washington Post,* 12 March 1995, p. A–21.

————. "U.S. Rebuffs Chinese Plea on U.N. Rights Vote," *Washington Post,* 2 March 1995, p. A–25.

Mydans, Seth. "Wife Urging Tough Response to Dissident's Arrest," *New York Times,* 10 July 1995, p. A–6.

"Mystery in China: Where is Dissident?" *New York Times,* 4 April 1994, p. A–3.

Oksenberg, Michel. "Heading Off a New Cold War with China," *Washington Post,* 3 September 1995, pp. C–1, C–3.

O'Neill, Mark. "China Urges U.S. Action to Repair Ties," *Washington Post,* 4 July 1995, p. A–17.

"Pakistan Denies Arms Report," *Washington Post,* 5 July 1995, p. A–19.

"Police in China Arrest Two More Dissidents," *New York Times,* 22 May 1995, p. A–5.

Protzman, Ferdinand. "Deals Offset Debate on China in Germany," *New York Times,* 6 July 1994, p. D–6.

Ray, Hemen. *China and Eastern Europe* (New Delhi: Radiant Publishers, 1988), 203 pp.

Randal, Jonathan C. "Sudanese Civil War Proves Resilient," *Washington Post,* 6 May 1995, p. A–20.

"Recognition from China," *New York Times,* 21 November 1988, p. A–11.

Richburg, Keith B. "China Bitterly Attacks Critics in U.S.," *Washington Post,* 24 August 1995, p. A–29.

———. "Hong Kong's Road to Chinese Rule Viewed as Poor Example for Taiwan," *Washington Post,* 17 June 1995, p. A–13.

———. "Modern Taiwan Looks Inward for New National Identity," *Washington Post,* 11 June 1995, p. A–26.

———. "One Giant Step Out of Isolation: President's 'Private' Trip to Cornell Reunion Hailed as Breakthrough in Taipei," *Washington Post,* 8 June 1995, pp. A–29, A–34.

———. "U.S. China to Resume Trade Talks," *Washington Post,* 7 February 1995, p. A–14.

———. "U.S. Embassy Aide Visits American Jailed in China," *Washington Post,* 10 August 1995, p. A–23.

Riding, Alan. "5 Powers Will Seek Ban on Major Mideast Arms," *New York Times,* 10 July 1991, p. A–9.

"Riyadh and Beijing Declare Start of Full Diplomatic Ties," *New York Times,* 22 July 1990, p. I–6.

Robert, Stephen. "Viewpoints: In China, Let Free Markets Aid Liberty," *New York Times,* 24 April 1994, p. III–11.

Rondinelli, Dennis A., editor. *Expanding Sino-American Business and Trade: China's Economic Transition* (London: Quorum Books, 1994), 270 pp.

Rosenbaum, David E. "China Trade Rift with U.S. Deepens," *New York Times,* 29 January 1995, pp. 1, 8.

Rosenthal, A. M. "On My Mind: Clinton's Honor Saved!" *New York Times,* 13 May 1994, p. A–31.

———. "On My Mind: For a China Boycott," *New York Times,* 30 August 1994, p. A–20.

———. "On My Mind: Fresh Air for America," *New York Times,* 21 June 1994, p. A–17.

———. "On My Mind: Who Pays China's Army?" *New York Times,* 5 August 1994, p. A–25.

Sanger, David E. "Chinese Invite U.S. to Resume Talks to Trade," *New York Times,* 7 February 195, pp. A–1, D–6.

———. "Christopher and Chinese Official Fail to Settle Differences," *New York Times,* 2 August 1995, p. A–3.

———. "In a Trade Pact with China, a Ghost of Japan," *New York Times,* 27 February 1995, pp. D–1, D–6.

———. "President Imposes Trade Sanctions on Chinese Goods," *New York Times,* 5 February 1995, pp. 1, 12.

———. "This Is a Trade War! Get Your Popgun!" *New York Times,* 12 February 1995, pp. IV–1, 5.

———. "Trade Fight Aside, U.S. to Sell China More Wheat," *New York Times,* 8 February 1995, pp. D–1, D–18.

———. "U.S. Threatens $2.8 Billion of Tariffs on China Exports," *New York Times,* 1 January 1995, p. 14.

Schichor, Yitzhak. "China and the Gulf Crisis: Escape from Predicaments," *Problems of Communism,* Vol. XL (November 1991), pp. 80–90.

Schmemann, Serge. "Mideast Momentum: Christopher Follows Well-Worn Path in Quest to Revive the Peace Effort," *New York Times,* 12 June 1995, p. A–2.

Sciolino, Elaine. "A Draft State Dept. Report Finds China's Rights Record Is Still Poor," *New York Times,* 12 January 1994, pp. A–1, A–5.

———. "Angered Over Taiwan, China Summons Home Its Ambassador," *New York Times,* 17 June 1995, p. 5.

———. "A Trade Tie That Binds," *New York Times,* 5 February 1995, pp. 1, 12.

———. "Beijing Rebuffs U.S. on Halting Iran Atom Deal," *New York Times,* 18 April 1995, pp. A–1, A–8.

———. "China Rejects Call from Christopher for Rights Gains," *New York Times,* 13 March 1994, pp. 1, 8.

———. "China's Prisons Forged Zeal of U.S. Crusader," *New York Times,* 10 July 1995, pp. A–1, A–6.

―――. "China Trip Begins on a Frosty Note for Christopher," *New York Times*, 12 March 1994, pp. 1, 4.

―――. "Christopher Ends Beijing Talks Citing Modest Gains," *New York Times*, March 1994, p. A–3.

―――. "Christopher Unlikely to Meet Dissidents," *New York Times*, 11 March 1994, p. A–10.

―――. "C.I.A. Report Says Chinese Sent Iran Arms Components," *New York Times*, 22 June 1995, pp. A–1, A–6.

―――. "Clinton and China: How Promise Self-Destructed," *New York Times*, 29 May 1994, pp. 1, 8.

―――. "Clinton Rejects Penalizing China," *New York Times*, 26 May 1994, pp. A–1, A–8.

―――. "Conflicting Pressures on Clinton Mount over China's Trade Status," *New York Times*, 20 May 1994, p. A–9.

―――. "In Warning to U.S., China Cracks Down on 2 Dissidents," *New York Times*, 29 June 1995, p. A–8.

―――. "In a Box: In China, Not Quite a Year after a Trade Compromise, Human Rights Issues Fester," *New York Times*, 16 January 1994, p. IV–2.

―――. "State Dept. Study Says China Lags on Human Rights," *New York Times*, 1 February 1995, pp. A–1, A–6.

―――. "So Friendly: Chinese and Christopher: Secretary Offers Praise in Jakarta," *New York Times*, 12 November 1994, p. 6.

―――. "Sourly, Christopher's Talks in Beijing Come to an End," *New York Times*, 15 March 1994, p. A–3.

―――. "U.S. Lifts Its Sanctions on China over High-Technology Transfers," *New York Times*, 22 February 1992, pp. 1, 5.

―――. "U.S. May Threaten Chin with Sanctions for Reported Arms Sales," *New York Times*, 20 July 1993, p. A–3.

―――. "U.S. Moves to Ease Beijing Sanctions," *New York Times*, 8 March 1994, p. A–8.

―――. "U.S. Says It Warned Wu about Earlier Trip to China," *New York Times*, 14 July 1995, p. A–6.

―――. "U.S. Showing Frustration over China's Human Rights Policy," *New York Times*, 9 March 1994, p. A–11.

―――. "U.S. to Try a Conciliatory Tack with China," *New York Times*, 23 March 1994, p. A–12.

————. "Winston Lord: Where the Buck Stops on China and Human Rights," *New York Times,* 27 March 1994, p. 8.

————. "White House Gets Progress Report on Rights in China," *New York Times,* 24 May 1994, pp. A–1, A–6.

Segal, Gerald. "Beijing's Fading Clout," *New York Times,* 25 May 1994, p. A–21.

Seymour, James D. "Human Rights in China," *Current History* Vol. 93, No. 584 (September 1994): pp. 256–259.

"Shanghai Dissidents Held," *New York Times,* 9 April 1994, p. 4.

"Shanghai Dissidents Reportedly Jailed," *New York Times,* 12 October 1994, p. A–3.

Shenon, Philip. "Prison Sentences Seem Likely in Trial of 14 Chinese Dissidents," *New York Times,* 24 July 1994, p. 15.

————. "Conversations/Zhu Muzhi: Want to Sell China's Record on Human Rights? Get Mr. Smooth," *New York Times,* 28 August 1994, p. IV–7.

Sieff, Martin. "Anger at U.S. Brings China, Russia Closer: Resentment Centers on Human Rights," *The Washington Times,* 3 July 1995, pp. A–1, A–8.

————. "China Recalls Envoy to U.S.; Aims to Head Off Opening to Taiwan," *The Washington Times,* 17 June 1995, pp. A–1, A–14.

————. "Separating Trade, Rights Fails to Improve China," *The Washington Times,* 15 January 1995, pp. A–1, A–16.

————. "U.S. Probes China on Missiles: Pakistan Sale May Trigger Sanctions," *The Washington Times,* 4 July 1995, pp. A–1, A–8.

"Speak Louder on Rights in China," *New York Times,* 29 August 1994, p. A–14.

Smith, Craig S. "Major Firms in U.S.–China Trade Says Sanctions by U.S. Wouldn't Hurt Much," *Wall Street Journal,* 7 February 1995, pp. A–2, A–12.

————. "U.S. Envoy Leaves China with Little to Show on Rights," *Wall Street Journal,* 16 January 1995, p. A–10.

————. "U.S.-China Deals Shrink under Scrutiny," *Wall Street Journal,* 15 August 1995, p. A–13.

Smith, R. Jeffrey. "Iran's Missile Technology Linked to China, Report Says," *Washington Post,* 17 June 1995, p. A–14.

————, and David B. Ottaway. "Spy Photos Suggest China Missile

Trade: Pressure for Sanctions Builds over Evidence That Pakistan Has M-11s," *Washington Post,* 17 June 1995, pp. A–1, A–17.

———. "U.S. Accuses China of Germ Weapons Work," *Washington Post,* 15 July 1995, p. A–18.

Southerland, Daniel. "First Private Visit to U.S. Completed, Taiwan President Mulls Trip to Alaska," *Washington Post,* 11 June 1995, p. A–26.

———. "Lee Visit Turns into a Balancing Act," *Washington Post,* 10 June 1995, p. A–8.

"The Puzzling Infirmity of America's Small Firms," *The Economist,* 18 February 1995, pp. 63, 64.

"Tiananmen and China's Future: The View Five Years Later," *Current History* No. 93, Vol. 584 (September 1994), pp. 247–49.

"Top China Dissident Is Reported Released," *New York Times,* 3 April 1994, p. 6.

Triplett, William C. 2nd. "Dangerous Embrace," *New York Times,* 10 September 1994, p. 19.

Tyler, Patrick E. "Abuses of Rights Persist in China Despite U.S. Pleas," *New York Times,* 29 August 1994, pp. A–1, A–2.

———. "As Deng Fades, China's Leaders Tighten Grip on Power," *New York Times,* 19 December 1994, p. A–3.

———. "Awe-Struck U.S. Executives Survey the China Market," *New York Times,* 2 September 1994, pp. D–1, D–2.

———. "Beijing Arrests Rights Defender," *New York Times,* 9 July 1995, pp. 1, 10.

———. "Beijing Is Warning Leading Dissident," *New York Times,* 27 February 1994, p. 4.

———. "Beijing Journal: A Dissident Finds the Political Prospects Bleak," *New York Times,* 16 April 1994, p. 4.

———. "Beijing Says It Could Live Well Even if U.S. Trade Was Cut Off," *New York Times,* 21 March 1994, pp. A–1, A–10.

———. "China Agrees to Resume Talks with U.S. on Human Rights," *New York Times,* 31 August, 1994, p. A–2.

———. "China Allows a Prominent Dissident to Leave," *New York Times,* 11 May 1994, p. A–12.

———. "China Arrests Leading Dissident for the Second Time in a Month," *New York Times,* 2 April 1994, pp. 1, 4.

————. "China Arrests Petitioner for Democracy," *New York Times*, 20 May 1995, p. 4.

————. "China Calls on Clinton for Stand on Taiwan," *New York Times*, 13 July 1995, p. A–8.

————. "China Detains and Then Frees a Top Dissident," *New York Times*, 5 March 1994, pp. 1, 4.

————. "China Dissident, Hoping to Meet Christopher, Is Detained at Home," *New York Times*, 13 March 1994, p. 8.

————. "China Dissident Reports Release," *New York Times*, 6 March 1994, p. 12.

————. "China May Allow Red Cross to Visit Dissidents in Jail," *New York Times*, 10 November 1993, pp. A–1, A–17.

————. "China Moves Ahead on Huge but Disputed Dam," *New York Times*, 27 December 1994, p. A–3.

————. "China Promises U.S. to Try to Improve Its Human Rights," *New York Times*, 16 January 1994, pp. 1, 9.

————. "China Releases Dissident and Sends Him to U.S. for Treatment," *New York Times*, 24 April 1994, p. 6.

————. "China Says a Top Dissident Is Not Being Held but Has Left Beijing," *New York Times*, 8 March 1994, p. A–12.

————. "China Says It Holds Dissident to Check 'New Crimes,' " *New York Times*, 5 April 1994, p. A–6.

————. "China's Discus Champ: Alone, Disabled and Barred," *New York Times*, 8 September 1994, p. A–3.

————. "China's Hidden Army of Workers Strives to Adapt," *New York Times*, 11 December 1994, p. 3.

————. "China's Hidden Army of Workers Strives to Adapt," *New York Times*, 11 December 1994, p. 3.

————. "China: Slower Growth, Still Spectacular," *New York Times*, 3 January 1994, p. C–9.

————. "China Sees Risk to Its Stability in U.S. Demands," *New York Times*, 19 May 1994, pp. A–1, A–10.

————. "China Warns against 'Star Wars' Shield for U.S. Forces in Asia," *New York Times*, 18 February 1995, p. 4.

————. "China Welcomes U.S. Trade Policy," *New York Times*, 28 May 1994, pp. 1, 5.

153

————. "Chinese Aide Conciliatory Despite 'Foolish' U.S. Stand on Rights," *New York Times,* 11 March 1995, p. 5.

————. "Chinese Crackdown: Challenge Is Still Prohibited," *New York Times,* 7 March 1994, p. A–8.

————. "Chinese Dissident Appears; May Meet Christopher," *New York Times,* 10 March 1994, p. A–11.

————. "Chinese Dissident Facing Possibility of New Charges," *New York Times,* 6 April 1994, p. A–12.

————. "Chinese Hit by Tank Is Denied Place in Games," *New York Times,* 2 September 1994, p. A–5.

————. "Chinese Puzzle: After Months of Dialogue on Human Rights, Beijing Takes Harder Line toward the U.S.," *New York Times,* 14 March 1994, pp. A–1, A–3.

————. "Chinese Take Journalists on Guided Tour of Prison," *New York Times,* 6 March 1994, p. 12.

————. "Clinton Is Expected to Strengthen the Diplomatic Status of Taiwan," *New York Times,* 10 August 1994, p. A–7.

————. "Crossroads for China: With Democratic Stirrings among Chinese, U.S. Is Pressing Beijing on Crucial Choices," *New York Times,* 29 January 1994, pp. 1, 4.

————. "Discontent Mounts In China, Shaking the Leaders," *New York Times,* 10 April 1994, p. 3.

————. "Eye on Olympics, China Frees Top Dissident," *New York Times,* 14 September 1993, p. A–6.

————. "Highest U.S. Rights Official Meets with Leading Chinese Dissident," *New York Times,* 28 February 1994, p. A–2.

————. "In a Surprise Gesture, China Releases a Major Dissident," *New York Times,* 14 May 1994, p. 7.

————. "Is China Stumbling?", *New York Times,* 6 February 1995, pp. A–1, A–11.

————. "Is Top Dissident Even Alive? Beijing Will Not Say," *New York Times,* 31 March 1995, p. A–10.

————. "New Dispute Imperils Trade with Chinese," *New York Times,* 12 March 1995, p. 21.

————. "Old Soldier May Take Deng's Mantle," *New York Times,* 15 May 1995, p. A–6.

———. "On Anniversary, Tiananmen Leader Speaks Out," *New York Times,* 5 June 1995, p. A–3.

———. "Rights in China Improve, Envoy Says," *New York Times,* 1 January 1994, p. 5.

———. "Scientists Urge Beijing to Stop Its Persecutions," *New York Times,* 16 May 1995, pp. A–1, A–12.

———. "Sidetracking Rights, U.S. Aide Pursues Business in China," *New York Times,* 30 August 1994, p. A–6.

———. "The Dynamic New China Still Races against Time," *New York Times,* 2 January 1994, p. IV–4.

———. "The U.S.–China Slide," *New York Times,* 23 May 1995, p. A–10.

———."Tough Stance Toward China Pays Off for Taiwan Leader," *New York Times,* 29 August 1995, pp. A–1, A–8.

———. "U.S. and China in a Clash over Human Rights," *New York Times,* 2 march 1995, p. A–7.

———. "U.S. and China Plan Meeting of Their Leaders in October," *New York Times,* 28 August 1995, pp. A–1, A–2.

———. "U.S. Envoy to China Is Reported Preparing to Leave Post Early," *New York Times,* 11 June 1995, p. 8.

———. "U.S., Praising China, Is Still Wary on Rights," *New York Times,* 13 October 1993, p. A–15.

———. "Visit by Gore to China Is Under Study," *New York Times,* 20 December 1994, p. A–3.

———. "6 Years After the Tiananmen Massacre, Survivors Clash Anew on Tactics," *New York Times,* 30 April 1995, p. 12.

———. "7 Chinese Intellectuals Appeal for End to Political Repression," *New York Times,* 11 March 1994, pp. A–1, A–10.

———. "12 Chinese Intellectuals Call for Limit on Police Powers," *New York Times,* 3 March 1995, p. A–2.

———. "12 Intellectuals Petition China on Corruption," *New York Times,* 26 February 1995, pp. 1, 6.

Tyson, Laura. "Taiwan Investors Unaffected by Chinese Sabre-Rattling," *Financial Times,* 25 July 1995, p. 5.

"U.N. Rights Panel Declines to Censure China," *New York Times,* 9 March 1995, p. A–5.

155

"U.S. Can't Budge China on Human Rights," *Washington Times,* 16 January 1995, p. A–15.

"U.S., China Clash on Dissident," *Washington Post,* 5 July 1995, p. A–19.

"U.S., China Discuss Problems," *Washington Post,* 27 August 1995, p. A–25.

"U.S. Determines China Violated Pact on Missiles," *New York Times,* 25 August 1993, pp. A–1, A–7.

"U.S. Protests Misdirection on Activist in China," *Washington Post,* 4 July 1995, p. A–17.

"U.S. Urged to Shift China Policy on Trade," *New York Times,* 30 January 1994, p. 3.

"U.S. Won't Pull China's MFN for Arresting Activists," *Washington Times,* 17 July 1995, p. A–15.

"Victors in the Struggle among China's Leaders," *New York Times,* 25 June 1989, p. 10.

Walker, Tony, and Bernard Gray. "Spy Case Threatens Sino–U.S. Ties," *Financial Times,* 10 July 1995, p. 1.

Walker, Tony. "U.S. Business Alarm Grows over China Chill," *Financial Times,* 10 July 1995, p. 5.

Weber, Bruce. "Detour on Journey to Democracy," *New York Times,* 3 June 1995, pp. 21, 22.

Wei Jingsheng. "A Hostage to the Olympics," *New York Times,* 1 March 1994, p. A–23.

Weiner, Tim. "Prisoner's Case Strains U.S.–China Ties," *New York Times,* 11 July 1995, p. A–8.

Weymouth, Lally. "The Peace Wheel Should Move: Egypt's Mubarak Nudges Israel and the PLO toward Compromise," *Washington Post,* 11 June 1995, p. C–2.

Whitney, Craig R. "France Proposes New, 'Last-chance' Peace Conference on Bosnia," *New York Times,* 1 February 1995, p. A–11.

———. "U.S. and 4 Other Big Arms Makers Adopt Guidelines on Sales," *New York Times,* 20 October 1991, p. 11.

"Wife Makes Plea for Jailed Chinese Official," *New York Times,* 15 May 1994, p. 20.

Wines, Michael. "In House, Tirade on China, but a Vote to Keep Trade as It Is," *New York Times,* 21 July 1995, p. A–3.

Wu, Yu-Shan. "Taiwan in 1993: Attempting a Diplomatic Breakthrough," *Asian Survey,* Vol. 34, No. 1 (January 1994), pp. 46–54.

WuDunn, Sheryl. "An Urbane Technocrat: Jiang Zemin," *New York Times,* 25 June 1989, p. 10.

————. "China Sentences an Ex-Official to 7 Years Over Tiananmen Leaks," *New York Times,* 22 July 1992, p. A–3.

————. "Israel Agrees to Ties with China, Aiding Beijing Role in Talks," *New York Times,* 24 January 1992, p. A–9.

Zhang Jia-lin. *China's Response to the Downfall of Communism in Eastern Europe and the Soviet Union,* Essay No. 48 (Hoover Institution on War, Revolution, and Peace: Stanford University, 1994), 26 pp.

Zweig, David. "Clinton and China: Creating a Policy Agenda That Works," *Current History* Vol. 92, No. 575 (September 1993), pp. 245–52.

"4 Seized in Peking Pasting Up Posters," *New York Times,* 5 April 1994, p. A–14.